mangia
with
QUATTRO

mangia with QUATTRO

FAMILY-STYLE ITALIAN FROM THE HEART

ANTONIO CORSI

WITH PATRICK CORSI AND TANIS TSISSEREV

whitecap

Whitecap Books

Whitecap Books is known for its expertise in the cookbook market, and has produced some of the most innovative and familiar titles found in kitchens across North America. Visit our website at www.whitecap.ca.

Editing: Lesley Cameron
Proofreading: Joan E. Templeton
Design: Michelle Mayne
Photography: Hamid Attie
Old family photos courtesy of Antonio Corsi
Recipes on pages 208, 210, 212, 216, 219, 221, 222, 224 and 225 by Merri Schwartz
Textured background design by Topic Concept Design Inc. (Vancouver)

Printed in China

Library and Archives Canada Cataloguing in Publication

Corsi, Antonio, 1950–

    Mangia with Quattro / Antonio Corsi, Patrick Corsi, Tanis Tsisserev.

ISBN 978-1-55285-982-7

    1. Cookery, Italian. 2. Quattro (Restaurant). I. Corsi, Patrick, 1974– II. Tsisserev, Tanis III. Title.

TX723.C66 2009   641.5945   C2009-902680-5

The publisher acknowledges the financial support of the Government of Canada through the Book Publishing Industry Development Program (BPIDP) and the Province of British Columbia through the Book Publishing Tax Credit.

09 10 11 12 13   5 4 3 2 1

This book is dedicated in loving memory to my papà, Giovanni Corsi.

CONTENTS

THIS PAGE My papà, Giovanni, with my younger brothers, Claudio and Massimo, 1968.
OPPOSITE PAGE Me on the first day of first grade, 1956.

INTRODUCTION

Our family has always enjoyed the important things in life: cooking food made with fresh, seasonal ingredients; sharing simple meals with friends; drinking joyously and living with *abbondanza*. *Abbondanza* is Italian for abundance and passion for life – it's Italian for being Italian! And it's the most important ingredient in every recipe in this book.

Mangia with Quattro: Family-Style Italian from the Heart brings together a lifetime's worth of restaurant and family recipes, anecdotes and experiences. I was working on this book during the summer of 2008 when my entire family visited from Italy and Germany for three weeks. It was a wonderful time. Many stories, lots of laughter and fond memories were shared across the table, while we feasted on many of the recipes included in these pages.

THIS PAGE (Clockwise from top left): My son, Patrick, overlooking my home town of Maenza; salute!; Park Hotel Adler in Germany (that's me in the middle); flambé time; one of my early jobs as a waiter in Rome. OPPOSITE PAGE: Me with my granddaughter.

Many of you will turn to this book because you've come to know the Corsi family over a meal at Quattro throughout the years, and that's great – this book is definitely for you! It's also for anyone who knows first-hand the joy of turning up the music loud enough to feel it in your bones and preparing a beautiful, indulgent meal for family and friends.

"Abbondanza" is Italian for abundance and passion for life – it's Italian for being Italian! And it's the most important ingredient in every recipe in this book.

I came by my love of food and family naturally. I'm Italian, after all. I was born in Maenza, a small town outside of Rome, and grew up there with my four brothers and one sister. My mother passed away when I was 18 years old, and my father looked after us all on his own. He died in 2007. Papà, this book is for you.

I trained as a chef and worked in the kitchens and dining rooms of various hotels and restaurants throughout Europe. In 1968 I moved to Hinterzarten, Germany, to work at one of Europe's finest hotels, the Park Hotel Adler. Most nights my buddies and I would go for drinks after work at a nearby restaurant where I made a point of paying no attention to the hotheaded and beautiful woman behind the bar. One night, tired of being ignored, she poured a drink over me. That's how I met Edith. We've been married now for over 35 years. Our son, Patrick, is now my business partner. Our daughter, Ida, and her husband, Albert, have two wonderful little girls, Sofia and Amaya, who are the lights of my life.

When Edith and I came to Canada with the children in 1976, we settled in North Vancouver. My older brother, Mario, lived here already and we worked together at the Park Royal Hotel, earning ourselves quite a reputation.

Mario and I went on to open four restaurants, but Corsi Trattoria, which we opened in 1980, has always had a special place in my heart. We specialized in making all our own pasta, using only semolina and eggs, and we were the only restaurant in those days to have – and use! – a pasta maker. It was truly a family business as Edith and I practically raised our children at the restaurant.

Twenty years later, Patrick and I returned to the site of Corsi Trattoria to open Gusto di Quattro. Edith still enjoys overseeing the restaurant at lunch.

In 1993 we opened Il Portico in Edmonton. We were basking in Il Portico's success when, in the summer of 1994, I received a late-night phone call from Patrick.

"Dad, it's time to go big in Vancouver," he said. "Let's open the restaurant we've always dreamed of."

I flew to Vancouver immediately. Within 72 hours the ink was dry on the lease of 2611 West Fourth Avenue in Vancouver, the home of Quattro on Fourth. Why "Quattro," people ask me all the time. Although I claim I'm not superstitious, the number four seems to be lucky for me. I was born on the fourth day of the fourth month; it was 1994 when we opened the restaurant and I was 44 years old; there were four partners at the time; and I had just won $444 on a lotto ticket.

Today Quattro on Fourth continues to thrive just as well as its sister restaurants Gusto and Quattro at Whistler.

For this book I've chosen a selection of recipes from every chapter in my life. They're meant to be enjoyed family-style with the people you care about. Edith says she wishes I were a one-pot cook at home, but to me, cooking is all about the experience, the sizzle and the steam. I like to have four pots and one great conversation going all at once. I can spend hours in the kitchen, loving every minute of it.

"Mangia, mangia con gusto e un augurio di buona salute!"

— **ANTONIO CORSI**

THIS PAGE (Clockwise from top left): In Venice in 1964; with Chef Hans Shaub (centre) and my brother Mario (right) at Park Royal Hotel in West Vancouver in 1977; the dining room and bar at Quattro on Fourth; with Edith in Hinterzarten in 1968; as a waiter in Rome. OPPOSITE PAGE: Me with my son, Patrick.

My nephew Giovanni, with his father, Mario (my oldest brother)

A TASTE OF HEAVEN

My weekends are usually pretty busy, but the weekend before my 26th birthday I found myself with no plans. I decided to make the most of my time and drove up to Whistler to hang out with my Uncle Antonio. He was working at Quattro that night, so I met him at the restaurant and we spent the night chatting about life and family. I'll always remember this special night as it's one of the few times that we've spent together without anyone else around. But I will also remember the meal. Oh lord, the meal!

I'm a red meat fan and I felt like indulging in a good steak for my birthday, so Antonio recommended the beef tenderloin. When it arrived, I found myself gazing at a thing of beauty. It was a carnivore's dream: fantastic tenderloin with the perfect amount of caramelized onions, drizzled with a rich, dark balsamic reduction. It looked almost too good to eat but I ate it anyway.

I'll always remember my first bite. If heaven has a flavour, this would be it. All conversation stopped for me as I lost myself in my meal. My enjoyment was absolute. Antonio then opened a bottle of 1994 Caymus Special Selection – and it took the tenderloin to a whole new level. How much did I enjoy this food and wine pairing? All I'll say is that I spent 45 minutes to finish my meal. No word of a lie, 45 minutes. You don't rush perfection.

I shook Chef Jeremie Trottier's hand afterward and thanked him for giving me one of the greatest meals I have ever had. A decade later I still talk about the beef tenderloin I had at Quattro Whistler for my birthday. I'll never forget it. Over the years, I've ordered it again and it's always been spectacular, but like the old saying goes, "you never forget your first taste of heaven."

— GIOVANNI CORSI

ROMAN PANTRY
Dispensa

We're claiming artistic licence with the Italian translation here because there's no word for pantry in Italian. In fact, there's no such thing. Everything is fresh, bought the day of. But for my modern household I always have certain types of pasta, cheeses, herbs, stocks, sauces, vegetables, oils and vinegars on hand to make meal preparation simple, fast and, yes, fresh. Whether it's from scratch or off the store shelf, make sure you have at least chicken and veal broth on hand most of the time. They're used in a lot of recipes here.

Anchovies are one of my very favourite ingredients. They're the secret touch in many Mediterranean recipes. I love them because they add so much depth and complexity to simple foods. So do as the Romans do, and make sure to stock some.

PASTA

Bucatini
Fettuccine
Fusilli
Lasagna
Linguine
Penne rigate
Rigatoni
Spaghetti

MEAT

Guanciale
Pancetta
Prosciutto

VEGETABLES

Arugula
Carrots
Celery
Garlic
Dry mushrooms: chanterelle, porcini
Onions
Peas (frozen)
Potato
Rapini
Shallots
Tomato: fresh and canned

CHEESE

Bocconcini
Buffalo mozzarella or fresh mozzarella
Caciocavallo
Goat cheese
Gorgonzola
Parmesan
Pecorino Romano
Ricotta

FRESH HERBS

Basil
Cilantro
Chives
Italian parsley
Mint
Oregano
Rosemary
Sage
Thyme

DRIED HERBS & SPICES

Basil
Bay leaf
Coriander seeds
Cumin seeds
Curry powder
Nutmeg
Oregano
Peppercorns: white, black, pink
Saffron
Spanish paprika
Thyme

STOCKS

Veal (page 11)
Chicken (page 10)
Fish (page 12)
Vegetable (page 14)

SAUCES

Cream (page 16)
Pesto (page 18)
Tomato (page 15)

OILS & VINEGARS

Aged balsamic vinegar
Balsamic vinegar
First press or extra virgin olive oil for raw dishes
Red wine vinegar
Regular olive oil for cooking
White wine vinegar

WINE & SPIRITS

Brandy
Cognac
Dry red wine
Dry white wine
Marsala
Port
Vermouth

OTHER

Amarena cherry syrup
Anchovies
Arborio rice
Breadcrumbs: regular and Panko
Canned beans: cannellini, black turtle
Canned tuna
Capers
Chili flakes
Cornmeal
Dijon mustard: smooth and grainy
Dried figs
Nuts: pine nuts, walnuts, hazelnuts, pistachios
Olives
Peperoncino
Semolina flour
Sun-dried tomatoes
Tomato paste
Truffle oil
Truffle paste

A good stock is the foundation ingredient in many recipes, and I encourage you to try making some of these stocks at least once. You'll see that I've included freezing instructions so that you can whip up a big batch to keep in the freezer. Otherwise, you can find terrific organic, low-sodium choices at most grocery stores.

CHICKEN STOCK
Brodo di Pollo

5 lb chicken bones
24 cups water
4 cloves garlic
2 medium onions, chopped in 2-inch pieces
2 medium carrots, chopped in 2-inch pieces
1 bunch celery, chopped in 2-inch pieces
2 sprigs thyme
2 sprigs sage
1 bay leaf
1 Tbsp whole black peppercorns
1 tsp salt

Makes 20 cups

Combine all the ingredients in a large stockpot and bring to a boil. Skim off any fat and impurities that rise to the surface. Reduce the heat to low and gently simmer, partially covered, for 2 to 3 hours.

Strain the stock through a fine-mesh sieve and cool.

This stock may be frozen for up to 6 months.

To freeze the stocks and sauces in this chapter, place the freshly made stock or sauce in a cold water bath to cool it quickly, stirring frequently. Divide the sauce into freezer containers when it's cool.

VEAL STOCK
Brodo di Vitello

5 lb veal marrow bones, split
½ cup tomato paste
½ lb carrots, chopped in
  2-inch pieces
½ lb onions, chopped in
  2-inch pieces
8 stalks celery, chopped in
  2-inch pieces
8 cloves garlic
2 cups dry red wine
1 bay leaf
1 Tbsp black peppercorns
2 sprigs sage
2 sprigs thyme
2 sprigs rosemary
1 bunch parsley
28 cups of water

Makes 20 cups

Preheat the oven to 350°F.

Roast the veal bones for 2 hours. Remove them from the oven, brush with the tomato paste and return them to the oven to brown for 30 minutes.

Add the vegetables to the roasting pan with the bones and brown for another 30 minutes.

Remove the pan from the oven and transfer the bones and vegetables to a stockpot. Deglaze the roasting pan with the red wine then add the liquid to the stockpot. Add the bay leaf, peppercorn, fresh herbs and water. Bring to a boil then reduce the heat and simmer gently, partially covered, for 6 to 7 hours.

Strain the stock through a fine-mesh sieve and cool.

This stock may be frozen for up to 6 months.

To make demi-glace, reduce the veal stock by three-quarters of its volume, or until it turns a deep, thick colour.

FISH STOCK

Brodo di Pesce

5 lb fish bones (of white fish)
24 cups water
1 cup dry white wine
3 stalks celery, chopped in
    2-inch pieces
1 onion, chopped in 2-inch
    pieces
1 bulb fennel, chopped in
    2-inch pieces
1 bunch parsley
1 sprig thyme
1 bay leaf
1 Tbsp white peppercorns
1 tsp salt

Makes 20 cups

Combine all the ingredients in a large stockpot and bring to a boil. Skim off any fat and impurities that rise to the surface. Reduce the heat to low and gently simmer, partially covered, for 30 to 40 minutes.

Strain the stock through a fine-mesh sieve and cool.

This stock may be frozen for up to 6 months.

VEGETABLE STOCK
Brodo di Verdure

2 lb button mushrooms,
  roughly chopped
1 bunch celery, roughly
  chopped
2 medium onions, roughly
  chopped
4 cloves garlic
2 medium carrots
2 sprigs thyme
2 sprigs sage
1 sprig rosemary
1 bunch parsley
1 bay leaf
24 cups water
1 tsp salt

Makes 20 cups

Place all the ingredients in a large stockpot. Bring to boil then reduce the heat.
  Simmer gently, partially covered, for 2 hours.
  Strain the stock through a fine-mesh sieve and cool.
  This stock may be frozen for up to 6 months.

BASIC TOMATO SAUCE
Salsa al Pomodoro

3 Tbsp extra virgin olive oil
1 cup diced onion
1 extra-large can (100 fl oz)
    whole Italian tomatoes
3 Tbsp tomato paste
1 Tbsp dried oregano
2 tsp dried basil
1 tsp salt
¼ cup salted butter
¼ cup all-purpose white flour

Tomato sauce is the little black dress of Italian cooking. **Makes about 12 cups**

Heat the olive oil in a large soup pot over low heat. Sweat the onion – the slower the better to bring out its natural sugars, about 5 minutes. It should be meltingly tender before you add the tomatoes and tomato paste. Simmer over low heat for 1 hour, stirring occasionally and breaking up any large pieces of tomato with the back of a spoon. Add the oregano, basil and salt.

Make a roux in a separate small saucepan by melting the butter over low heat and slowly whisking in the flour. Cook over low heat for 5 to 6 minutes, stirring constantly. Whisk the cooked roux into the hot tomato sauce and simmer for 10 minutes.

This sauce may be frozen for up to 6 months. (See sidebar, page 10.)

CREAM SAUCE
Salsa alla Crema

4 cups whipping cream
1 lb cream cheese
1 tsp grated nutmeg
½ tsp salt
White pepper

I cannot tell a lie—there's nothing light about this cream sauce. But it's worth the indulgence. **Makes 6 cups**

In a saucepan, very slowly bring the whipping cream and cream cheese to a boil. Whisk frequently to prevent the cream cheese from burning. Add the nutmeg, salt and a pinch of white pepper.

Strain the sauce through a fine-mesh sieve. If it's too thick, add a little bit of water to thin the consistency.

This sauce may be frozen for up to 6 months.

MEAT SAUCE
Ragù di Carne

¼ cup extra virgin olive oil
1 cup finely diced onion
¼ cup pancetta, small dice
2 cloves garlic, crushed
½ cup finely diced celery
½ cup finely diced carrot
1 cup chopped fresh
   chanterelle mushrooms (if
   you can't find chanterelles,
   use button mushrooms)
1 sprig rosemary + 2 sprigs
   sage, tied together
2 cups chicken stock (page 10)
1½ lb ground beef
1½ lb ground veal
1 cup dry red wine
4 cups tomato sauce (page 15)
¼ cup tomato paste
Salt
Ground black pepper
1 cup grated Parmesan cheese
¼ cup chopped Italian parsley

I come back to this recipe again and again. **Makes 10 cups**

In a large saucepan, heat the olive oil. Add the onion and pancetta, and sweat until the pancetta is crisp, 4 to 5 minutes. Stir in the garlic, celery and carrot and cook for 2 to 3 minutes. Add the mushrooms with the rosemary-sage bouquet and cook, stirring, for 2 minutes.

Deglaze the pan with the chicken stock, and reduce it until almost all the stock has evaporated. Add the beef and veal. Cook for 5 minutes. And the red wine and cook for another 5 minutes.

Add the tomato sauce and tomato paste and simmer over low heat for 30 to 40 minutes. Remove the rosemary and sage bouquet. Season to taste with salt and pepper then sprinkle with the Parmesan and Italian parsley.

This sauce may be frozen for up to 6 months.

When fresh basil is available in the summer, it's an excellent addition at the end for a fresh, clean flavour.

PESTO | *Pesto*

Pesto can be used in so many ways. Try it in soup (it's ideal on minestrone and perfect with mushroom), slip some inside a chicken breast or use it to perk up scrambled or poached eggs at breakfast. A simple pesto pasta is great with my Brick-Flattened Cornish Game Hen (page 145).

BASIL PESTO
Pesto al Basilico

8 oz fresh basil leaves
¼ cup pine nuts
2 cloves garlic, peeled
1 cup extra virgin olive oil, divided
½ cup grated Parmesan cheese
Salt
Ground black pepper

Makes 2 cups

Preheat the oven to 350°F.

Wash the basil and discard the stems.

Lightly toast the pine nuts for 6 to 8 minutes then let them cool.

In a food processor, purée the garlic with ½ cup of the olive oil. Add the basil leaves, cooled pine nuts and remaining olive oil. Pulse until the mixture has a coarse consistency then add the Parmesan cheese with the motor running. Scrape the pesto into a bowl, and season to taste with salt and pepper if necessary.

Excess pesto can be frozen in ice cube trays or small baggies until needed.

ARUGULA PESTO

Pesto alla Rucola

2 cups firmly packed arugula
   leaves, tough stems
   discarded
⅓ cup walnuts
½ cup extra virgin olive oil,
   divided
Salt
Ground black pepper

Makes about 1 cup

Pulse the arugula, walnuts and half the olive oil in a food processor. With the motor running, drizzle in as much of the remaining oil as necessary until the mixture has a coarse consistency.

   Remove and season to taste with salt and pepper.

HOMEMADE PASTA DOUGH

Pasta Fatta in Casa

¾ cup semolina flour
¾ cup all-purpose white flour
7 free-range eggs (I like Vita Eggs), lightly beaten

This basic recipe really is worth a try. **Makes ¾–1 lb**

Place both flours in the bowl of a stand mixer. Using the dough hook on low speed, slowly add the lightly beaten eggs until a dough starts to form. Transfer the dough from the bowl onto a clean, lightly floured board and work it for 2 minutes.

Alternatively, place the flour on a clean work surface and form a well in the centre. Add the eggs to the centre and bring in the flour from the sides with your hands to make the dough.

Wrap the dough in plastic wrap and refrigerate it for at least 1 hour. Remove it from the fridge and roll it to the required thickness in a pasta machine or by hand.

BASIC RISOTTO

Base per Risotti

4 cups hot chicken stock
  (page 10)
2 Tbsp salted butter
2 Tbsp finely diced shallots
2 cups arborio rice
½ cup dry white wine
¼ cup grated Parmesan
  cheese (or more)
2 Tbsp butter (or more)
Salt
Freshly ground black pepper

Is there any other way to cook rice? In this recipe you can partially cook the risotto ahead of time so you can bring it out of the fridge when you need it and finish cooking it with extra stock. **Serves 6**

Keep the chicken stock hot in a saucepan on the stovetop.

Melt the butter in a heavy-bottomed pan and sweat the shallots over medium heat until softened, about 1 minute. Add the rice and stir for 2 minutes until the rice grains are all coated with butter. Add the white wine and cook until all the wine has evaporated, 2 to 3 minutes.

Increase the heat to medium-high and add 2 cups of the hot chicken stock. Stir every minute for the next 8 minutes until the stock has almost gone. Add 1 more cup of chicken stock and stir more frequently so the risotto doesn't stick to the bottom of the pan. Bite into a grain of rice to see if it is almost al dente, but not starchy. Add small amounts of the remaining stock as necessary until it's nearly al dente.

Spread the risotto out on a tray to cool, then refrigerate until needed.

To finish cooking, you'll need about another 8 minutes and ½ cup more chicken stock. When the risotto has cooked, add the Parmesan cheese, butter, salt and freshly ground pepper, all to taste.

Serve hot.

SOUPS AND SALADS
Zuppe e Insalate

EGG SOUP

Stracciatella

8 cups cold chicken stock,
   divided (page 10)
6 egg yolks
Juice of 1 lemon
1 Tbsp finely chopped fresh
   marjoram
Salt
Ground black pepper
½ cup grated Parmesan
   cheese

It wouldn't be an Italian cookbook without an egg soup recipe. **Serves 6**

Bring 7 cups of the chicken stock to a boil in a large saucepan.

In a bowl, beat together the egg yolks, lemon juice and remaining 1 cup of cold chicken stock. Transfer this to a separate soup pot. Whisking constantly, slowly add the warm chicken stock in a steady stream to the egg yolk mixture and place over medium heat. Continue whisking as the broth just comes to a boil. When there is steam rising from the centre and tiny bubbles around the edges of the broth, remove it from the heat immediately. The soup will be smooth and creamy yellow.

Add the fresh marjoram and season to taste with salt and pepper. Ladle the soup into warm soup bowls and garnish with grated Parmesan cheese.

BREAD SOUP

Zuppa di' Pane

1 loaf rustic Italian bread,
   a few days old
8 cups chicken stock (page 10)
1 cup tomato sauce (page 15)
1 tsp peperoncino
½ cup grated pecorino Romano
2 Tbsp chiffonade of fresh
   basil

I just love bread soup, and a stale, rustic Italian bread is the perfect excuse to make it. Three-day-old bread is ideal. Fresh bread absorbs too much liquid and the crumbs lack the texture you need for this dish. **Serves 6–8**

Cut the bread into ½-inch pieces.

In a large saucepan, bring the chicken stock, tomato sauce and peperoncino to a boil over medium-high heat. Add the bread pieces to the boiling mixture, whisking constantly until the bread pieces have a foamy texture.

Remove the saucepan from the heat and whisk in the cheese. Garnish with fresh basil just before serving.

MINESTRONE

Minestrone alla Ida

½ cup extra virgin olive oil
1 lb green cabbage, chopped (1 small cabbage)
1 lb spinach, well washed, stemmed, chopped (about 1½ bunches)
1 cup diced onion
½ cup diced celery
½ cup diced carrot
16 cups chicken stock (page 10) or vegetable stock (page 14)
3 cups canned tomatoes, drained, chopped (reserve juice)
One 4 oz Parmesan rind
½ lb spaghettini, broken into 2-inch pieces
Salt
Ground black pepper
1 small bunch fresh basil, cut in chiffonade
1 cup grated Parmesan cheese

I make this recipe a little differently each time. Sometimes I'll add potatoes, sometimes cannellini beans and sometimes short pasta, like broken spaghetti noodles. The slow cooking with the vegetables was my sister Ida's idea, and it enhances the soup's true vegetable flavour. **Serves 10 (or more)**

In a large soup pot, heat the olive oil on low heat and slowly sweat the cabbage, spinach, onion, celery and carrot, covered, for 45 minutes to 1 hour. The vegetables will release their juices and soften without colouring.

Add the stock, tomatoes and Parmesan rind, cover and bring to a boil. Once it's boiling, add the pasta, reduce the heat and simmer for 12 to 15 minutes. Season to taste with salt and pepper. Discard the Parmesan rind.

Garnish with fresh basil and a sprinkling of Parmesan cheese. Serve hot.

This soup may be frozen for up to 6 months. To freeze it, place the soup in a cold water bath to cool it quickly, stirring frequently. Divide the soup into freezer containers when it's cool.

POTATO AND MUSHROOM SOUP
Zuppa di Patate e Funghi

2 Tbsp extra virgin olive oil
2 stalks celery, cut in ¼-inch dice
1 carrot, cut in ¼-inch dice
1 medium onion, cut in ¼-inch dice
1 clove garlic, finely chopped
2 lb fresh wild mushrooms, cleaned, sliced
2 oz dry porcini mushrooms, soaked in warm water for 20 minutes, drained and liquid reserved, chopped
4 cups veal stock (page 11) or chicken stock (page 10)
1 cup diced Yukon Gold potatoes (½-inch dice)
¼ cup finely chopped chives, divided
¼ cup chopped Italian parsley, divided
2 tsp finely chopped fresh thyme
Salt
Ground black pepper

This is my dear friend Jeremie Trottier's creation. Jeremie is the chef at Quattro at Whistler. This soup is always the first thing Edith requests when we get to Whistler. **Makes 6–7 cups**

In a large soup pot over medium-high heat, add the olive oil, celery, carrot, onion and garlic. Sweat the vegetables for 2 to 3 minutes. Stir in the wild and porcini mushrooms and sauté for 5 to 10 minutes.

Add the stock, potatoes, reserved mushroom water, half the chopped chives, half the parsley and half the thyme. Season to taste with salt and pepper. Cover and simmer for 30 to 40 minutes, or until the potatoes are cooked. Let rest for 5 minutes.

Stir the remaining herbs into the hot soup and serve.

ZUCCHINI AND FENNEL SOUP

Zuppa al Finocchio

ZUCCHINI AND FENNEL SOUP

¼ cup butter

2 lb zucchini, peeled and
  chopped in ½-inch dice

1 medium onion, cut in ½-inch
  dice

1 bulb fennel, core removed,
  cut in ½-inch dice

2 cloves garlic, puréed

1½ tsp salt

1 tsp ground coriander

1 tsp dried basil

1 tsp dried oregano

¼ cup all-purpose white flour

8 cups chicken stock (page 10)

1 cup whipping cream

2 Tbsp liquid honey

Salt

Ground black pepper

EGGPLANT CROSTINI

1 large eggplant

1 tsp extra virgin olive oil +
  extra for brushing on crostini

Salt

½ cup grated Parmigiano
  Reggiano

2 Tbsp fresh oregano

Ground black pepper

6–8 pieces crusty Italian
  bread, cut into ½-inch-thick
  pieces

It's hard to believe now but I was practically a vegetarian until I was about 12 years old. My favourite foods were figs and fennel. I could usually be found munching on a piece of fennel straight from Papà's *giardino*. **Serves 6–8**

For the soup, melt the butter in a large saucepan over medium heat and sweat the zucchini, onion, fennel and garlic for 4 to 5 minutes. Add the salt and spices and cook for a further minute. Add the flour to form a roux and cook, stirring constantly, for 2 minutes. Slowly add 4 cups of the chicken stock and bring to a boil. Add the remaining stock and return to a boil.

Add the cream, bring to a boil again, reduce the heat to medium-low and simmer for 25 minutes, stirring frequently to prevent the soup from burning on the bottom of the pot. Allow the soup to cool slightly, then purée in a blender. Add the honey and season to taste with salt and pepper.

While the soup cooks, make the crostini.

Preheat the oven to 400°F. Line a baking pan with tinfoil.

Roll the eggplant in the 1 tsp olive oil. Score the skin of the eggplant and heavily salt its outside. Place it in the prepared baking pan and roast it for 45 minutes, or until a skewer goes into flesh very easily.

Remove the cooked eggplant from the oven, split it in half lengthwise and scoop the flesh into a bowl. Mix in ¼ cup of the grated cheese, the oregano, pepper and more salt to taste.

Toast the bread lightly. Brush 1 side with some of the extra olive oil and spread the eggplant mixture overtop. Sprinkle the remaining cheese over each crostino.

To serve, pour the hot soup into warm soup bowls and float an eggplant crostino on top of each serving.

SMOKED CHICKEN, CORN AND POTATO CHOWDER

Pollo inzuppato

SPICE MIX

2 Tbsp ground or whole
   coriander seeds
1 Tbsp dried thyme
1 tsp dried basil
1 tsp dried oregano
1 tsp salt

SOUP

½ cup salted butter
2 jalapeño peppers, finely
   diced, seeds discarded
1 medium onion, cut in
   ½-inch dice
1½ cups celery, cut in
   ½-inch dice
½ cup all-purpose white flour
4 cups chicken stock (page 10)
2 lb Yukon Gold potatoes,
   peeled, cut in ½-inch dice
1 lb smoked chicken, cut in
   ½-inch pieces
1 lb corn kernels, fresh or
   frozen
1 cup whipping cream (36%)
1 bay leaf
Juice of 2 limes
1 Tbsp chopped fresh cilantro
   per bowl

Try to use Yukon Gold potatoes in this comforting, cream-based soup. For the smoked chicken, ask the deli for extra-thick slices. Roasted chicken also works. **Serves 6–8**

Grind the spice mix ingredients in a mini processor or coffee mill for 1 minute. Set aside.

For the soup, melt the butter in a large soup pot on medium heat. Sweat the jalapeños, onion and celery in the butter for 4 minutes. Add the spice mix to the pot and stir to mix well. Reduce the heat to low and add the flour. Cook, stirring constantly, for 2 minutes. Slowly stir in the chicken stock and bring to a boil.

Add the potatoes, chicken, corn, cream and bay leaf. Bring to a boil and reduce the heat to a simmer. Continue cooking until the potatoes are tender. Squeeze the limes into the soup and mix to combine.

To serve, ladle the soup into warm soup bowls and garnish with cilantro.

GREEN SALADS WITH GOAT CHEESE | *Insalata con Caprino*

There were always goats in the pasture and greens in the garden when I was growing up in Italy. Here are a few of my favourite green-salad-with-goat-cheese combinations. *Buon appetito!*

GREEN SALAD WITH GOAT CHEESE AND APPLES
Insalata alla Mela

CROUTONS
3 slices 1-inch-thick Tuscan
   bread
Olive oil for brushing

DRESSING
⅔ cup extra virgin olive oil
⅓ cup balsamic vinegar
Salt
Ground black pepper

SALAD
8–10 cups mixed wild salad
   greens
2 Granny Smith apples,
   peeled, quartered, cored,
   thinly sliced
2 Red Delicious apples,
   peeled, quartered, cored,
   thinly sliced
1 cup seedless red grapes, cut
   in half
1 cup goat cheese, crumbled
½ cup shaved Parmesan
   cheese
½ cup hazelnuts, roasted

Serves 6–8

For the croutons, preheat the grill or a ridged pan on the stovetop.

Lightly oil the bread, and grill for 2 minutes on each side. Cut it into 1-inch croutons while it's still warm.

For the dressing, whisk together the oil and vinegar. Season to taste with salt and pepper.

For the salad, place the salad greens in a large bowl and add the apples, grapes, cheeses and hazelnuts. Toss these with the croutons to mix well. Just before serving, drizzle dressing over the greens to coat the salad lightly.

To serve, transfer the salad to a large platter or bowl.

To roast hazelnuts, place them on a baking sheet in a single layer. Roast for 10 or 15 minutes in a 350°F oven. Place them on a kitchen towel and let cool for 15 minutes, before rubbing them vigorously with the towel to remove the skins.

MIXED GREENS WITH SEARED GOAT CHEESE

Insalata Balsamica

VINAIGRETTE
¼ cup chopped shallots
½ tsp extra virgin olive oil
1 cup black olives, pitted and
    roughly chopped by hand (do
    not purée)
1 tsp Dijon mustard
1 cup extra virgin olive oil
¼ cup balsamic vinegar
2 sprigs oregano, leaves only
2 sprigs thyme, leaves only
¼ cup liquid honey
Pinch chili flakes

GOAT CHEESE
½ cup Panko breadcrumbs
½ tsp olive oil
2 sprigs oregano, leaves only
Salt
10 oz soft goat cheese, divided
    into 6 portions
Oil for searing

SALAD
Mixed salad greens (mesclun
    spring mix) for 6 portions

Serves 6

Sauté the shallots with the ½ tsp oil in a small pan until translucent. Cool. Combine the cooled shallots with the remaining vinaigrette ingredients in a small bowl and mix everything well by hand. This is not an emulsified dressing, so don't be concerned if the dressing separates. Set aside.

Place the breadcrumbs, olive oil, oregano and salt in a food processor and process until well mixed to make a crust mix for the cheese. Shape the goat cheese portions into pucks and roll them in the herb crust. Press the crust firmly into the cheese.

Preheat the oven to 400°F.

Brush an ovenproof non-stick pan with a little oil and place it over medium heat. Add the crusted goat cheese pucks and sear them on 1 side only. Flip them over and transfer the pan to the oven to bake the pucks for 3 to 4 minutes until the cheese has melted inside.

Toss the salad greens in a large bowl with enough vinaigrette to coat the leaves evenly then divide the leaves among 6 plates. Drizzle more vinaigrette around the salad. Carefully place a warm goat cheese puck on top of each serving and serve immediately.

RADICCHIO SALAD WITH GOAT CHEESE

Radicchio e Caprino

Serves 6

For the dressing, soak the cranberries in the cherry syrup to soften them. In a blender or food processor, blend the egg yolks for 1 minute to slightly thicken. Strain the cranberries, discard the cherry syrup, add half the cranberries to the egg yolks and blend for 30 to 40 seconds. (Reserve the other half of the cranberries.) Slowly drizzle in 1 cup of the vegetable oil while the machine is running. The mixture should thicken slightly.

While the blender is running add the vinegar, coriander and white pepper to taste. Add the shallot, mustard and lemon zest then season to taste with salt. While the blender is running drizzle in the remaining 1 cup of vegetable oil.

Preheat the broiler to medium-high with the rack set 6 to 8 inches below the heat source. Line a baking sheet with parchment paper.

Roll the goat cheese portions in the chopped pine nuts to coat all sides and transfer them to the prepared baking sheet. Broil for 2 to 3 minutes until the nuts are golden and the cheese has softened.

Mix the salad greens with enough dressing to lightly coat the leaves. Transfer them to a serving platter, top with the goat cheese and garnish with the remaining cranberries.

DRESSING

½ cup sun-dried cranberries, divided

½ cup Amarena cherry syrup (see recipe intro page 52)

4 egg yolks

2 cups vegetable oil, divided

⅓ cup Champagne vinegar

1 Tbsp ground coriander

White pepper

1 shallot, finely chopped

2 Tbsp Dijon mustard

Zest of 1 lemon

Salt

GOAT CHEESE

6–8 oz log of goat cheese, cut into 1-inch portions

½ cup pine nuts, hand-chopped

RADICCHIO SALAD

2 heads radicchio

3 heads butter lettuce

ORANGE AND FENNEL SALAD

Finocchio all' Arancia

2 bulbs fennel
4 large oranges, segmented
¼ cup extra virgin olive oil
Juice of ½ lemon
Salt

This is perfect with Dungeness Crab and Sea Scallop Cakes (page 43). **Serves 6–8**

Wash the fennel, then trim off and discard the stalks. Cut each bulb in half, remove the core and shave the bulbs thinly on a mandolin. In a salad bowl, toss the fennel gently with the orange segments, olive oil and lemon juice. Add salt to taste.

CAPRESE SALAD

Insalata Caprese

6 vine-ripened tomatoes
6 balls bocconcini
Salt
Ground black pepper
¼ cup extra virgin olive oil
2 Tbsp chiffonade or whole
  leaves of fresh basil

This is always a favourite at the restaurants. It's tastiest in summer when tomatoes are at their peak. **Serves 6**

Slice each tomato and bocconcini ball crosswise into three ½-inch slices. Alternate the tomato and bocconcini slices in a circular pattern on a serving plate.

Season to taste with salt and pepper, drizzle with the olive oil and garnish with the basil.

CUCUMBER SALAD

Cetrioli e Pomodorini

2 long English cucumbers
1½ cups grape tomatoes
Salt
Ground black pepper
½ cup extra virgin olive oil
¼ cup white wine vinegar
3 Tbsp chiffonade of fresh
    basil (optional)

This is a great picnic dish that's even better the next day. **Serves 6 (or more)**

Peel the cucumbers and halve them lengthwise. Scoop out the seeds with a spoon or a melon baller, cut the cucumber crosswise in ¼-inch slices and place the pieces in a bowl.

Remove the tiny tops from the grape tomatoes and split them in half lengthwise. Add them to the cucumber slices.

Season to taste with salt and pepper. Add the oil and vinegar, and fresh basil, if desired. Toss together and serve.

CHICKEN SALAD WITH ARUGULA

Insalata di Pollo e Rucola

2 stalks celery, cut in 1-inch dice

1 carrot, cut in 1-inch dice

½ medium onion, cut in 1-inch dice

1 Tbsp whole black peppercorns, tied in cheesecloth

2-inch piece fresh ginger, peeled and thinly sliced

3 chicken breasts, 6–7 oz each, boneless, skinless

¼ cup extra virgin olive oil

3 Tbsp apple cider vinegar

Salt

¾ lb baby arugula, cut in chiffonade

2 celery hearts, leaves and tender stalks only, cut in chiffonade

Edith loves arugula and she eats salad all the time. This is one of her favourites. **Serves 6–8**

Bring 4 cups of water to a boil, reduce the heat to medium and add the celery, carrot, onion, peppercorns and ginger. Simmer, partially covered, for 30 minutes to infuse the vegetable flavours into the water. Add the chicken breasts and poach them gently for 10 to 15 minutes, until the juices run clear yellow when pricked with a fork. Remove the chicken and let it cool. Remove, drain and reserve the vegetables. Keep the stock to use in a soup.

Purée the reserved vegetables with the oil and vinegar to make a dressing. Season to taste with salt, if necessary.

Place the arugula and celery hearts on a large plate. Slice the chicken and fan it over the salad. Pour the dressing over the chicken and serve.

APPETIZERS
Appetitosi Stuzzichini

DUNGENESS CRAB AND SEA SCALLOP CAKES

Granchio e Ventaglio

½ lb scallops

4 oz white fish (cod, sablefish or halibut)

1 lb fresh crab meat

1 small red bell pepper, finely diced

1 jalapeño, finely diced, no seeds

3 Tbsp finely diced red onion

Juice of 1 lemon

1 Tbsp Worcestershire sauce

2 tsp Tabasco sauce, or to taste

1 egg

½ cup mayonnaise

½ cup arugula, chopped

1 Tbsp dried mustard powder

1 day-old Italian loaf or baguette, crusts off, turned into breadcrumbs

Salt

Panko breadcrumbs

Extra virgin olive oil

This recipe comes from our executive chef at Quattro at Whistler, my dear friend Jeremie Trottier. The secret to this recipe is to use only the freshest ingredients. Do your shopping on the day you plan to cook this. Orange and Fennel Salad (page 33) is a nice match. **Makes 16 crab cakes, serves 8 as a starter**

Purée the scallops and white fish in a food processor, then transfer them to a large stainless steel bowl.

Squeeze the crab meat to remove any excess moisture, then add it to the puréed fish with the red pepper, jalapeño, onion, lemon juice, Worcestershire sauce, Tabasco sauce, egg, mayonnaise, arugula and mustard powder. Combine everything well and add just enough Italian breadcrumbs to hold the mixture together.

Fry a small spoonful of mixture in some olive oil and taste. Add salt to taste if necessary before you continue cooking.

Preheat the oven to 400°F. Line a baking tray with paper towel.

Form the fish mixture into ¼-cup cakes and coat with the Panko crumbs. Heat ⅛ inch of the olive oil in an ovenproof pan over medium-high heat. Fry the crab cakes on 1 side only until they're golden brown. Flip the crab cakes over, transfer the pan to the oven and bake the crab cakes for 5 to 8 minutes, or until both sides are golden brown.

Place the cooked crab cakes on the prepared baking tray to blot up any excess oil, then transfer to a large platter. Serve with Orange and Fennel Salad (page 33).

SCALLOPS WITH PRAWN VANILLA BEAN BISQUE

Ventaglio Vanigliato

SCALLOPS

16 large scallops
3 Tbsp extra virgin olive oil
Juice of 1 lemon
¼ cup finely chopped Italian
    parsley + extra for garnish
Salt
Freshly ground white pepper
16 pieces thinly sliced cold-
    smoked BC salmon (lox)

PRAWN VANILLA BEAN BISQUE

1 lb prawn shells
2 carrots, roughly chopped
2 stalks celery, roughly
    chopped
1 onion, roughly chopped
¼ cup tomato paste
2 Tbsp brandy
4 cups water
1 vanilla bean, slit and seeds
    scraped
½ cup whipping cream
Salt
Ground black pepper

Wow! This is a great dish, and it's heavenly with a glass of really cold white wine. What better way to express yourself in a modern Italian restaurant than with west coast ingredients like salmon and scallops? Don't be intimidated. The recipe sounds complicated but it's quite simple to prepare. **Serves 8**

Marinate the scallops in the olive oil, lemon juice, parsley, salt and pepper for up to 1 hour in the fridge.

While the scallops are marinating, make the bisque.

Preheat the oven to 400°F.

Put the prawn shells, carrots, celery and onion in a shallow flameproof roasting pan and roast for about 25 minutes until the shells have turned pink and the vegetables are slightly caramelized. Transfer the pan from the oven to the stovetop over medium heat and stir in the tomato paste, coating all the ingredients as much as possible. Deglaze the pan with the brandy, stirring up all the brown bits from the bottom of the pan.

Transfer the ingredients from the pan to a large saucepan and add the water and vanilla bean seeds and pod. Reduce this over medium heat for about 30 minutes until it's a rich brown colour and slightly thickened. Remove the vanilla pod and strain the sauce through a fine-mesh sieve. Add the whipping cream and reduce the sauce further until it thickens some more. Season to taste with salt and pepper.

Remove the scallops from the marinade and wrap a slice of smoked salmon around each one. Fasten the salmon slices with toothpicks.

Heat a non-stick sauté pan over medium-high heat and sear the scallops for about 4 minutes on each side. Serve immediately by placing 2 cooked scallops in a warm shallow bowl and spooning the bisque around the base. Garnish with Italian parsley.

GRILLED CALAMARI STEAK

Calamari Piccanti con Capperi

CALAMARI

6 large tubes of calamari
  (about 6–7 oz each)
1 Tbsp baking soda
Salt
Ground black pepper
Cayenne pepper (optional)

MARINADE

¼ cup vegetable oil
3 Tbsp chopped Italian parsley
1 Tbsp chopped garlic
1 tsp cayenne pepper, or to
  taste
1 tsp ground black pepper, or
  to taste

SPICY TOMATO AND CAPER
SAUCE

1 Tbsp olive oil
2 anchovy fillets
¼ cup diced onion
3 Tbsp capers
1 tsp peperoncino
½ cup dry white wine
2 ripe Roma tomatoes, peeled,
  seeded, cut in ½-inch dice
  (½ cup tomato concasse)
1 cup tomato sauce (page 15)
Olive tapenade (page 60)

This isn't your regular deep-fried calamari recipe. It's a very earthy and delicious dish. If you have some pesto in the house (or you feel like whipping up some of your own, page 18) and you want to dress up the presentation, simply dot some around the platter. **Serves 6**

Tenderize the calamari by boiling it in plenty of water with the baking soda for ½ to 1 hour. Test it for tenderness after 30 minutes.

Meanwhile, prepare the marinade by simply combining the marinade ingredients in a non-reactive bowl that's big enough to hold the calamari.

Remove the calamari from the water and baking soda, drain it and place it in the marinade for at least 2 hours. The longer the better for this one, though.

For the tomato and caper sauce, heat the olive oil in a saucepan over medium heat and sauté the anchovies, onion, capers and peperoncino for 3 minutes. Add the white wine and tomato concasse, and cook until the volume has reduced by half. Add the tomato sauce and simmer for 15 to 20 minutes on low heat.

Preheat the grill to medium-high.

Remove any excess oil from the calamari with a paper towel to help avoid any flare-ups on the grill.

Season the calamari with salt and pepper to taste, adding cayenne pepper for extra spiciness, if desired.

Place the calamari on the grill and put a weight on top of them (a cast iron pan could work well) to help prevent shrinking. Grill for 4 minutes on each side, remove to a cutting board and slice them on an angle into thin pieces.

Arrange the calamari slices on a platter, spoon sauce around (but not on top of) the calamari and spoon some olive tapenade on top.

TEMPURA BC SPOT PRAWNS

Gamberetti Fritti

PRAWNS

18 large BC spot prawns
1 jalapeño pepper, seeds
  discarded, cut in fine dice
Zest of 1 lemon, finely
  chopped
Zest of 1 lime, finely chopped
Juice of ½ lemon
Vegetable oil for frying
All-purpose white flour for
  dusting
Salt
Lemon wedges

TEMPURA BATTER

1¼ cups all-purpose white
  flour
1 tsp salt
12 fl oz can cold sparkling
  soda water

BC's spot prawns are some of the most delectable treasures from the sea. There's even a local festival to celebrate them. Get your prawns fresh from the dock and enjoy these crispy morsels with an ice cold beer. **Serves 6**

Remove the shells from the prawns, leaving the tails on. Freeze the shells to use them in stock (or in the recipe on page 44). Butterfly the prawns 1½ inches along their back and discard the veins. Combine the jalapeño, citrus zests and juice in a non-reactive bowl. Add the prawns, cover and marinate in the fridge for 2 hours.

Meanwhile, make the batter. Place the flour and salt in a stainless steel bowl. Add the cold soda water and whisk until smooth. Cover and let rest in the fridge for 1 hour before using.

Heat the oil in a deep fryer to 350°F. Line a baking tray with paper towel.

Remove the prawns from the marinade and dust them in flour. Holding each one by the tail, dip them in the cold tempura batter. Deep-fry them in the hot oil in batches until they're golden brown, 1 to 2 minutes. Do not crowd the pan. Remove the prawns to the prepared tray, and sprinkle them immediately with salt to absorb the excess oil and to keep the prawns crisp.

Serve with lemon wedges.

SWORDFISH CARPACCIO

Carpaccio al Pesce Spada

12 oz swordfish fillet
½ tsp olive oil
1 Tbsp pink peppercorns, ground
¼ cup vermouth
¾ cup extra virgin olive oil, divided
1 onion, cut in julienne strips
Sea salt
½ cup radicchio, cut in chiffonade
½ cup arugula, cut in chiffonade

This is a perfect starter because it does just what it's supposed to do: it revs up your taste buds for the main course. It's a very well-balanced dish, and the fish, radicchio and arugula chiffonade all taste beautifully fresh. **Serves 6**

Slice the swordfish on a 15-degree angle into 6 thin slices. Place the slices between sheets of waxed paper and pound to a ¼-inch thickness.

Brush an ovenproof serving platter with a light coating of olive oil. Remove the top sheet of waxed paper from the fish and flip it onto the platter, fanning the pieces of fish out and overlapping them slightly, leaving the centre of the plate empty.

Sprinkle the fish with the ground peppercorns then drizzle with the vermouth and half the olive oil. Sprinkle the onion evenly overtop then cover the fish with plastic wrap and marinate in the fridge for 30 minutes.

Preheat the broiler.

Remove the fish from the fridge and discard the onion. Broil the swordfish for 2 minutes about 6 inches from the element.

Drizzle the fish with the remaining olive oil, season to taste with salt and top it off with the radicchio chiffonade. Pile the arugula in the centre of a serving plate, add the swordfish and serve.

MUSHROOM CARPACCIO
Carpaccio Sottobosco

1 cup white wine (Pinot Grigio works well)
2 Tbsp chopped fresh basil
1 Tbsp chopped garlic
1 tsp chili flakes
¼ cup olive oil
4 large portobello mushrooms, gills and stems removed
3 oz Asiago cheese, shaved
2 Tbsp white truffle oil
3 Tbsp torn fresh basil leaves
Salt
Ground black pepper

This is a very elegant vegetarian starter. **Serves 6**

Combine the wine, basil, garlic, chili flakes and olive oil in a non-reactive bowl. Add the mushroom caps and marinate them for 30 minutes, or until they're slightly soft.

Preheat the grill or a ridged pan on the stovetop.

Remove the mushrooms from the marinade and grill them for 2 to 3 minutes per side. When the mushrooms are cooked, stack one on top of the other on a plate and let them cool slightly. Cover them in plastic wrap, place a 4–5 lb weight on top and chill them for 2 hours in the fridge. Remove the weight, discard the liquid and transfer the mushrooms to the freezer until they're firm and chilled, about 1 hour.

Remove the mushrooms from the freezer and slice them very thinly. Arrange the slices on a large platter. Don't worry if you have a few broken slices.

Garnish the mushrooms with the Asiago cheese, a drizzle of white truffle oil and torn basil leaves. Season to taste with salt and pepper.

SHRIMP AND SWEET CORN RISOTTO WRAPS
Verza con Gamberetti

CABBAGE ROLLS

12 Savoy cabbage leaves, about 8 inches across
2 cups cooked risotto (page 21)
½ lb cooked baby shrimp
¾ cup sweet corn, fresh or frozen
1 Tbsp finely chopped fresh thyme
½ cup grated Parmesan cheese
¼ cup chicken stock (page 10)
Salt
Ground black pepper

BROTH

3 cups chicken stock (page 10)
2 pinches saffron (the better the quality the less you need)
1 bay leaf

GARNISH

2 ripe Roma tomatoes, peeled, seeded, cut in ½-inch dice (½ cup tomato concasse)

This is an Italian's tribute to cabbage rolls. It was inspired by the ever-popular Radicchio with Fresh Mozzarella (page 52), and they look beautiful when set side by side on an antipasto platter. **Makes 12 cabbage rolls**

For the cabbage rolls, drop the cabbage leaves into a large pot of boiling salted water for 4 to 5 minutes. Drain the cabbage well and let cool. The leaves should be pliable and easy to roll.

Mix the risotto with the baby shrimp, corn and fresh thyme. Add the Parmesan cheese, chicken stock and salt and pepper to taste.

Lay the cabbage leaves on a clean work surface. Cut out the thick stem in a V and trim the leaf if it's too large. Place about ¼ cup risotto in the centre of the leaf, closest to bottom edge. Roll the leaf forward to enclose the rice, folding the sides in as you do so to form a neat package. Place the rolls in a non-stick casserole or greased lasagna pan, seam side down. Repeat with the remaining leaves.

Preheat the oven to 400°F.

Bring the broth ingredients to a boil in a clean saucepan, and pour it over the cabbage rolls. Bake, covered, for 25 to 30 minutes, or until the risotto is hot in the centre.

To serve, place the wraps in individual bowls and ladle saffron broth from the pan around the rolls. Garnish each with 1 to 2 tsp of the tomato concasse.

RADICCHIO WITH FRESH MOZZARELLA

Radicchio Bocconcini

SALAD

1 Tbsp + 1½ tsp chopped
  fresh thyme
1 Tbsp + 1½ tsp chopped
  fresh oregano
1 Tbsp + 1½ tsp chopped
  fresh basil
1½ tsp Spanish paprika
3 Tbsp extra virgin olive oil
Salt
Ground black pepper
Nine 2 oz balls fresh
  mozzarella, cut in half
9 slices shaved prosciutto, cut
  in half
18 large wilted radicchio
  leaves (see chef's tip below)
Endive leaves to garnish

SOUR CHERRY VINAIGRETTE

½ cup Amarena cherry syrup
½ cup red wine vinegar

This recipe is wonderful year round but it's particularly fun to prepare on the barbecue during summer. Fresh herbs are best, of course, but if you're using dried herbs, reduce the amount by half. Amarena cherry syrup is a pantry staple in our home. It's great in salad dressings or over vanilla ice cream. You can find it at your favourite gourmet store or Italian delicatessen. **Serves 6**

For the salad, combine the fresh herbs, paprika, olive oil, salt and pepper in a glass or stainless steel bowl. Add the mozzarella, cover and marinate in the fridge for at least 3 hours, or as much as overnight.

Remove the mozzarella from the marinade and tightly wrap each piece of cheese with 1 piece of the prosciutto. Position each radicchio leaf with the white spine to your right in the 3 o'clock position. Place the mozzarella bundle on the front edge of the lettuce and roll the bundle away from you while tucking in the edges.

To make the vinaigrette, in a large saucepan over medium heat bring the cherry syrup and vinegar to a boil, then lower heat to simmer and reduce by half.

Meanwhile, heat a grill pan or barbecue to medium-high heat and grill the radicchio-bocconcini bundles for 3 minutes on each side, or until you can feel the cheese beginning to soften. Place them in the saucepan with the cherry vinaigrette. Bring to a gentle boil then immediately reduce the heat and simmer for 3 minutes, constantly turning the radicchios until they're soft and well coated in the sauce.

To serve, position the endive leaves around the edge of a serving platter, arrange the radicchio-bocconcini bundles in the middle and drizzle with the warm vinaigrette.

Wilting the radicchio leaves makes them supple and easier to work with. Peel the outer leaves away from the core and let them sit out overnight. To keep the bundles tight during grilling, give them a squeeze to gently break their spines.

BEEF CARPACCIO

Carpaccio Senape

BEEF

14 oz best-quality beef
tenderloin, trimmed of all
fat and sinew, wrapped in
plastic wrap and frozen until
very firm, about 2 hours

AIOLI

1 Tbsp smooth Dijon mustard
1 tsp grainy Dijon mustard
2 egg yolks
½ cup vegetable oil
½ tsp fresh lemon juice
Splash of cognac
Salt
Ground black pepper

GARNISH

White truffle oil to drizzle
2 cups packed arugula, rolled
and cut in chiffonade
12 pieces shaved Parmesan
cheese

We've always had a version of beef carpaccio on the menu at Quattro, even before it became trendy. This one is tried and true. Use only the best and freshest beef from a trusted source. **Serves 6–8**

Remove the beef tenderloin from the freezer and discard the plastic wrap. Slice the beef as thinly and neatly as possible with an electric slicer or by hand with a very sharp carving knife. Arrange the slices in a circular pattern on a serving platter, cover with fresh plastic wrap and refrigerate until ready to serve.

For the aioli, in a food processor or stainless steel bowl, whisk together the mustards and egg yolks until the mixture starts to thicken. Slowly drizzle in vegetable oil while whisking constantly to form a thick mayonnaise. Add the lemon juice and cognac to taste, whisking well to combine. Season to taste with salt and pepper. Transfer the aioli to a plastic squeeze bottle with a small tip and keep it cold until you need it.

Remove the plates of carpaccio from the fridge, discard the wrapping and season with salt and pepper. Drizzle aioli across the beef in a checkerboard pattern, then drizzle with white truffle oil. Mound arugula chiffonade in the centre of each plate and finish with shaved Parmesan cheese.

STEAK TARTARE
Carne Cruda

18 oz best-quality beef
    tenderloin
2 egg yolks
2 Tbsp Dijon mustard
1 shallot, finely diced
1 clove garlic, minced
2 anchovy fillets, finely diced
1 Tbsp finely chopped capers
¼ cup vegetable oil
¼ cup extra virgin olive oil
1 Tbsp finely chopped Italian
    parsley
1 Tbsp Cognac
1 tsp caper brine
Tabasco sauce
Lea & Perrins sauce
Salt
Cracked black pepper
Assorted olives
Crostini
Parmigiano Reggiano, broken
    into pieces

I've been making this recipe for as long as I can remember. I developed it when I was working at my father-in-law's restaurant in the Black Forest in Germany, and people would line up around the block for it. Everyone wanted the recipe, but I'd always keep a little secret ingredient to myself. Until now, of course. Texture is key in this tartare. **Serves 6**

Hand-chop the beef into ⅛-inch cubes and refrigerate it until needed.

Make a dressing by whisking together the egg yolks and mustard until emulsified. Add the shallot, garlic, anchovies and capers and mix well. In a slow, steady stream, whisk in the vegetable and olive oils to achieve a thick mayonnaise-like dressing. Stir in the parsley, Cognac and caper brine. Season to taste with Tabasco sauce, Lea & Perrins sauce, salt and pepper.

Combine the dressing with the diced beef and serve with olives, crostini and pieces of Parmigiano Reggiano.

All your work surfaces and equipment must be scrupulously clean and the ingredients kept cold. Do not use eggs with cracks in their shells.

LAMB POPS WITH PROSCIUTTO AND BOCCONCINI

Costolette Scottadito

18 small lamb rib chops,
   bones Frenched
Salt
¼ cup all-purpose white flour
4 eggs, beaten
3 cups breadcrumbs made
   from stale Italian bread
Extra virgin olive oil for frying
6 slices prosciutto, each cut
   into 3 pieces
18 slices bocconcini, ½ inch
   thick
3 Tbsp salted butter

This dish is best enjoyed if you eat it with your fingers. Set out a large platter for your friends and gather 'round to watch the game. **Serves 6**

Wrap the chops in plastic wrap and pound them lightly. Season them with salt, dredge them in the flour, dip them in the egg and then coat them in the bread-crumbs.

Preheat the oven to 400°F.

Heat the olive oil on medium heat in a sauté pan and brown the chops in batches until they're a light golden colour. Once they're brown on both sides, place the chops on a rimmed baking sheet. Arrange a piece of prosciutto and a slice of bocconcini on top of each chop. Bake until the bocconcini melts, 6 to 8 minutes.

Remove the chops from the oven and top each one with ½ tsp salted butter for added richness before serving.

FIGS WITH GOAT CHEESE AND PROSCIUTTO

Fichi al Prosciutto

18 fresh figs
3 Tbsp liquid honey
6 Tbsp (3 oz) soft goat cheese
3 large, thin slices Italian
   prosciutto, sliced lengthwise
   in 3 pieces
4 cups baby arugula
1 Tbsp pistachio oil
Salt
Ground black pepper

There's really nothing quite like fresh figs, and there are countless wonderful ways to enjoy them. Try slipping a pistachio inside along with the cheese and honey, and feel free to skip the baking step. You can't go wrong with these ingredients. **Serves 6**

Preheat the oven to 375°F.

Make small X-shaped incisions in the bottom of each fig. You'll stuff them through the bottom, leaving the top and stem intact.

Using an espresso spoon, place ½ tsp honey and 1 tsp goat cheese into each fig and lightly squeeze them closed.

Cut each prosciutto strip in half for a total of 18 small pieces of prosciutto. Wrap the prosciutto around the figs and place them on a baking sheet. Bake for 10 to 15 minutes, until the figs are soft and the prosciutto is crispy.

In a bowl, toss the baby arugula with the pistachio oil and season to taste with salt and pepper. Place some salad in the centre of each of 6 plates and top with 3 figs per serving.

OLIVE TAPENADE

Tapenade all'Olivo

15 black olives, pitted, roughly chopped

15 green Bella di Cerignola olives, pitted, roughly chopped

3 Tbsp grated Parmesan cheese

2 Tbsp sun-dried tomato, soaked then drained well

2 Tbsp extra virgin olive oil

1 tsp Dijon mustard

1 tsp roughly chopped garlic

Olive tapenade is a staple in our home. It's great to have on hand for my favourite kind of company—unexpected. You can use it to dress up meat or fish, or spread it on crostini for a tasty snack. **Makes 1½ cups**

Place all the ingredients in a food processor and pulse until a thick paste is formed. If the mixture seems dry, add more olive oil, ½ tsp at a time, pulsing between additions.

Store, covered, in the fridge for up to 1 week.

CROSTINI | *Crostini Misti*

Here are some of my favourite ways to enjoy a classic Italian antipasto. These aren't really recipes (you'll see I haven't included quantities for ingredients), they're more like ideas for flavour combinations. Get creative and try your own combos. Mix, match and enjoy!

Start with rustic Italian bread, grilled or toasted and sliced ¾ inch thick. While the bread is warm, rub it with extra virgin olive oil and a garlic clove that's been split in half to release its natural oil.

OLIVE TAPENADE (PAGE 60)

SALMON CREAM | *Salmone Affumicato*

Spread mascarpone on the crostini and top each one with a slice of smoked salmon, chopped capers and fresh basil.

MUSSELS AND GOAT CHEESE | *Cozze al Caprino*

Spread goat cheese on the crostini and top each one with 2 smoked mussels and 1 tsp of jalapeño jelly.

LIVER AND BRANDY | *Fegatini di Pollo*

Sauté chicken liver in olive oil with onions and sage, and finish with a splash of brandy. Purée the mixture in a food processor and spread on the crostini.

CLASSIC | *Panzanella*

Mix tomato concasse (tomatoes that are peeled, seeded and cut in ½-inch dice) with fresh basil and olive oil. Place on the crostini.

BEANS | *Fagiolata*

In a food processor, purée cannellini beans with an anchovy fillet, Italian parsley, salt and a pinch of white pepper. Spread on the crostini and top with olive oil.

TRUFFLED EGGS | *Uova al Tartufo*

Caramelize onions and scramble eggs and place both on the crostini. Drizzle with truffle oil.

SEMOLINA CRACKERS

Semolina Croccante

1 cup + 1 Tbsp lukewarm
 water
½ tsp active dry yeast
1 tsp granulated sugar
½ cup + 1 Tbsp olive oil
2½ cups all-purpose white
 flour + extra flour for rolling
 dough
½ cup semolina flour (or equal
 volume of fine cornmeal if
 you can't find semolina flour)
1¼ tsp salt
Coarse salt

The semolina flour gives these gorgeous, golden crackers a faint sweetness. Serve them with Italian cheeses, nuts and dried fruit. **Makes about 40 crackers**

In a small bowl, combine 1 Tbsp of the lukewarm water with the yeast. Stir to dissolve it, then sprinkle the sugar overtop. Set the bowl in a warm place until the yeast foams and begins to rise to the surface, about 10 minutes.

Add the remaining 1 cup water and the oil. Transfer the ingredients to the bowl of a stand mixer fitted with dough hook, or into a large bowl if working by hand with a wooden spoon. Add the flours and 1¼ tsp salt, and mix until a smooth, slightly sticky but strong dough forms.

Wrap the dough tightly in plastic wrap and refrigerate it for several hours or overnight.

Preheat oven to 350°F. Lightly grease a baking pan.

Divide the dough into 3 pieces and cover them lightly with plastic wrap to keep them moist. Roll the dough, 1 piece at a time, on a clean, well-floured surface, until it's very thin and stretchy. Don't be afraid to keep adding flour! This will make transferring the dough to the baking sheet easier. When fully rolled, the cracker dough will be almost translucent and the thickness of a nickel.

Use a pizza wheel or sharp knife to cut the cracker dough into large triangles, 4 to 5 inches long. (A good measurement is the length between the base of your thumb and the tip of your index finger.)

Transfer the crackers to a baking sheet, sprinkle them with the coarse salt and bake them until they're golden all over, about 20 minutes. Keep a close eye on them toward the end of the baking time. You may need to remove the crackers on the edge of the tray before those in the middle are done.

Cool the crackers at room temperature on a rack.

These will keep in an airtight container for up to 10 days, but they're absolutely delicious on the day they are made!

FOCACCIA

Focaccia

3 cups + 3 Tbsp lukewarm
   water
2½ tsp active dry (not instant)
   yeast (or 1 packet)
1 tsp granulated sugar
½ cup + 1 Tbsp olive oil
1 Tbsp liquid honey
6 cups all-purpose white flour
2 Tbsp chopped fresh or 1 tsp
   dried rosemary
2 Tbsp chopped fresh or 1 tsp
   dried oregano
2 tsp salt
1 Tbsp + 1 tsp coarse salt

This focaccia is easy to throw together a couple of hours before dinner. The great flavour comes from the ingredients, not from hours and hours of kneading and rising! We use all-purpose white flour rather than a stronger bread flour to mimic the low-protein flours of Italy. **Makes 1 focaccia, serves up to 12 people**

Oil a 9- × 13-inch baking pan for a taller loaf, or a 10- × 17-inch rimmed baking sheet for a thin, crispy bread.

Pour 1 cup of the lukewarm water into a bowl. Sprinkle the yeast overtop and stir to dissolve it. Sprinkle the sugar over the yeast and water, and place the bowl in a warm spot (on top of the oven works well), until the yeast begins to foam and rise to the surface, about 10 minutes.

Add the remaining water, the ½ cup oil and honey to the bowl then transfer the ingredients into the bowl of a stand mixer fitted with a dough hook (or into a large bowl if you're mixing by hand).

Add the flour, half the rosemary, half the oregano and the 2 tsp salt, and mix. You'll need a large wooden spoon and a strong arm if you're mixing by hand. Also, adding the flour a few cups at a time makes mixing by hand easier.

The dough will be soft and slack, but keep mixing until it starts to shine and develop long, elastic strands when it's pulled. Scrape the dough onto the oiled pan. It will be very sticky. To help you spread it more easily, rub 1 tsp of olive oil between your hands. Push the dough to fill all the corners of the tray or pan.

Cover the pan loosely with a tea towel, transfer it to a warm spot and let the dough rise until it's doubled in volume and fills the sides of the pan, about 1¼ hours.

Preheat the oven to 425°F.

Using your fingers, gently push the dough all over to form pockets in it. Mix the remaining 1 Tbsp of olive oil with 1 Tbsp of water and pour this across the dough. Sprinkle it with the coarse salt and the remaining herbs.

Bake the bread at 425°F for 15 minutes to give it a boost, then reduce the heat to 400°F for a further 20 to 25 minutes. The focaccia is done when it has turned a deep gold colour all over and sounds hollow when tapped.

Remove the pan from the oven and let it cool on a rack.

Serve focaccia slices with a good olive oil and balsamic vinegar for dipping, or use them as a base for sandwiches and snacks.

PASTA, RISOTTO
AND POLENTA

Pasta, Risotto e Polenta

SPAGHETTI QUATTRO
Spaghetti Quattro

½ cup black turtle beans, uncooked (method following), or ¾ cup cooked
1 lb spaghetti
¾ cup extra virgin olive oil or enough to cover the bottom of a pan to ¼ inch
2 Tbsp roughly chopped Italian parsley
1 lb ground chicken breast
2 Tbsp finely minced garlic
2 tsp chili flakes
1 cup tomato sauce (page 15)
Salt

I created this recipe late one night after I'd been cooking for hours for everyone else. We used to call it Spaghetti Trasteverini, to honour its Roman roots, and provided a full description of it on the menu. It wasn't until we wrote "for Italians only," though, that it became wildly popular. I guess everyone wants to be Italian. This is by far the most requested recipe at our restaurants. My brother Mario still claims that this is his recipe. I'm happy to agree with him just to keep the peace. But we all know the truth. Right, Mario? **Serves 6**

If beans are uncooked pick over them and rinse them under cold running water. Place them in a bowl, cover them with water and soak them overnight in the fridge.

Drain the beans then add them to a saucepan, cover them with fresh water and bring to a boil. Simmer them for 20 minutes, or until cooked and tender. The cooking time will vary depending on the age of the beans. You should have ¾ cup of cooked beans.

Bring a large pot of salted water to a boil. Cook the spaghetti until al dente (package directions minus 2 minutes). Drain the spaghetti and set it aside.

Heat the oil in a sauté pan over high heat. Add the parsley and sauté it until it sizzles and is crisp. Reduce the heat to medium-high, add the chicken and cook, stirring constantly, for 3 minutes. Add the garlic, chili flakes and cooked black beans. Keep stirring for 2 minutes. Add the tomato sauce and stir the ingredients vigorously. Add a pinch of salt and the cooked pasta. Stir well and serve immediately in warm bowls.

If you're making this recipe for 6 people be sure to use a large enough sauté pan. Timing and temperature are key in this recipe so you need enough space to stir everything quickly.

SPAGHETTI WITH SAUSAGE, CABBAGE AND POTATOES
Spaghetti Ciociara

1 lb spaghetti
½ cup julienned large white
  onion
¼ cup extra virgin olive oil
4 pieces Italian sausage, about
  4 oz each, skin removed and
  chopped finely
2 cups julienned green
  cabbage
½ cup dry white wine
1 cup diced partly cooked
  potatoes (½-inch dice)
½ cup chicken stock (page 10)
¼ cup grated pecorino
  Romano

There was a farmhouse in a village near where I grew up. My father would go by it when he travelled on business from time to time, and whenever possible he stopped there to have this pasta. The sausage was homemade and the cabbage and potatoes came straight from the ground. It was delicious then, and still is, even with supermarket ingredients. **Serves 6**

Bring a large pot of salted water to a boil. Cook the spaghetti until al dente (package directions minus 2 minutes). Drain the spaghetti and set it aside.

In a large skillet over medium heat, sweat the onion in the extra virgin olive oil for 3 to 4 minutes. Add the Italian sausage and half-cook it, 2 to 3 minutes. Add the cabbage and cook for 2 minutes, then deglaze the pan with the white wine.

Add the potatoes and chicken stock and cook until the fat in the pan and the chicken stock emulsify to form a sauce. Add the cooked spaghetti and toss well to coat.

Finish with pecorino Romano and serve in warm bowls.

PINE MUSHROOM SPAGHETTI

Spaghetti Whistler

½ cup extra virgin olive oil

2 lb pine mushrooms, cleaned and thinly sliced

Pinch of salt

2 Tbsp finely chopped garlic

2 tsp chili flakes

2 cups chicken stock (page 10)

1 lb spaghetti

½ cup grated Parmesan cheese

3 Tbsp finely chopped Italian parsley

Ground black pepper

Oh, I can taste it right now! Pine mushrooms have such an amazing aroma—just like perfume. I used to brag about Italian porcini mushrooms until I tasted BC's pine mushrooms. This recipe is simplicity and seasonality at their best. **Serves 6–8**

In a large sauté pan heat the oil over medium heat. Add the pine mushrooms and sauté, stirring until they're golden brown. Stir in the pinch of salt. Add the garlic and chili flakes, cooking for another 1 minute. Add the chicken stock and reduce by half.

Bring a large pot of salted water to a boil. Cook the spaghetti until al dente (package directions minus 2 minutes). Drain the spaghetti, add it to the mushroom sauce and cook it until it's almost dry. Add the Parmesan and parsley. Toss well. Season to taste with more salt and freshly ground pepper.

Serve in warm bowls.

SPAGHETTI IN PARCHMENT PAPER

Spaghetti al Cartoccio

1 lb spaghetti

½ cup olive oil

2 cloves garlic, lightly crushed, stuck with a toothpick for easy removal

2–3 anchovy fillets, finely chopped

3 Tbsp finely chopped Italian parsley

3 cups tomato sauce (page 15)

1 tsp chili flakes

6 Roma tomatoes, peeled, seeded, cut in ½-inch dice (1½ cups tomato concasse)

½ cup sliced black olives

12 fresh basil leaves, torn

It's fun to watch people's reactions when this "pasta present" is served at the restaurant. As the parcel is opened and the aroma floats from table to table, people get curious and start talking. Even if they've already ordered or enjoyed their meal, they'll often just have to try this dish. Serve this on a rainy day to warm your soul. **Serves 6–8**

Bring a large pot of salted water to a boil. Cook the spaghetti until al dente (package directions minus 2 minutes). Drain the spaghetti and set it aside.

In a clean large saucepan over medium heat, warm the oil and sauté the garlic until it's golden brown. Remove it from the pan, discard and add the anchovies. Cook them until they've dissolved.

Stir in the Italian parsley. Don't be shocked when it sizzles! Add the tomato sauce and chili flakes and cook them for 3 minutes on high heat. Add the tomato concasse, olives and reserved spaghetti.

Cook the sauce and pasta for 3 minutes to combine the flavours and to reduce the sauce slightly. Cool for 5 minutes.

Preheat the oven to 450°F. Line a large rimmed baking sheet with parchment paper.

Pour the spaghetti and sauce on the prepared baking sheet and top it with the basil leaves. Bring the paper edges together, fold them and twist the ends to create a sealed package.

Bake for 10 minutes until the paper is golden brown. Transfer the package to a large platter and open it at the table.

SPAGHETTI PUTTANESCA

Spaghetti Puttanesca

1 lb spaghetti
2 Tbsp extra virgin olive oil
½ white onion, diced
4–6 anchovy fillets, finely chopped
¼ cup finely chopped black Italian olives
3 Tbsp finely chopped capers
1 cup chopped canned tomatoes
1 Tbsp finely chopped garlic
1 Tbsp chili flakes
1 bunch Italian parsley, finely chopped

This is a classic Roman pasta. I suspect that most people now know the origins of its name. The inexpensive ingredients were easily afforded by ladies of the night and could be prepared quickly and easily. **Serves 6**

Bring a large pot of salted water to a boil. Cook the spaghetti until al dente (package directions minus 2 minutes). Drain the spaghetti and set it aside.

While the spaghetti is cooking, heat a large skillet over medium heat. Add the olive oil and sweat the onion until it's softened but not browned. Add the anchovies, olives and capers and cook for 5 minutes.

Add the tomatoes, garlic, chili flakes and parsley. Simmer until the sauce thickens a little, 5 to 8 minutes.

Toss with the cooked, drained spaghetti and serve.

SPAGHETTI CARBONARA

Spaghetti Carbonara

1 lb spaghetti
1 onion, chopped
3 Tbsp butter
½ lb smoked pancetta,
   cut in julienne strips
½ cup dry white wine
4 eggs
½ cup grated Parmesan
   cheese + extra for serving
Ground black pepper

This is a very seductive pasta. And just like a good seduction, timing is everything. Be sure to read this recipe from start to finish and have all your ingredients at hand before you start to cook. **Serves 6**

Bring a large pot of salted water to a boil. Cook the spaghetti until al dente (package directions minus 2 minutes).

Heat a large skillet over medium-high heat and sweat the onion in the butter for 3 minutes. Add the pancetta and fry until it's crisp.

Deglaze the pan with the white wine and reduce the volume by three-quarters. Prepare your sauce so that it's nearly done when spaghetti is cooked.

Whisk the eggs in a serving bowl with the ½ cup Parmesan cheese and black pepper to taste. Add the hot cooked and drained pasta and mix everything together. Pour the pancetta and onion sauce overtop and mix again.

Finish with a lavish sprinkling of grated Parmesan cheese and serve.

SPAGHETTI WITH OLIVE OIL AND GARLIC

Spaghetti Aglio e Olio

1 lb spaghetti
½ cup extra virgin olive oil
2 Tbsp finely chopped garlic
1 whole dried red chili
Salt
2 Tbsp chopped Italian parsley

This is the kind of food that Italy is famous for. The secret of this dish is to start the sauce 3 to 4 minutes before the spaghetti is cooked. Timing and temperature are the keys to success in this recipe. **Serves 6**

Bring a large pot of salted water to a boil. Cook the spaghetti until al dente (package directions minus 2 minutes). Drain the spaghetti and set it aside.

In a skillet, heat the extra virgin olive oil over medium heat. Add the garlic and chili. When the garlic turns brown, remove the pepper and discard it. Add the cooked spaghetti and salt to taste. Sprinkle Italian parsley overtop and mix everything together quickly so the spaghetti can absorb the oil without it separating.

Do not be tempted to add any cheese to this dish.

SPAGHETTI WITH CHEESE AND PEPPER

Spaghetti Cacio e Pepe

1 lb spaghetti
8 cups warm chicken stock
  (page 10)
3 Tbsp pasta water (or more)
1 cup grated pecorino Romano
1 Tbsp coarse ground black
  pepper

This recipe is a pasta that thinks it's a risotto. Confused? My brother Claudio, sister Ida and I had a little competition going to see who could make the best *Spaghetti Cacio e Pepe*. I won with this recipe. Traditionally, the pasta is simply cooked in boiling salted water and drained, but in this recipe it's cooked like rice is in a risotto. **Serves 6**

Place the spaghetti in a large pot, add 2 cups of the warm chicken stock and cook over medium-high heat until the liquid is absorbed. Continue adding chicken stock until the pasta is al dente, about 15 minutes. It should be moist but not liquid. Pour the spaghetti into a warm pasta serving bowl and toss with the 3 Tbsp pasta water to moisten. Add the pecorino Romano and black pepper and toss.

Serve immediately.

SPAGHETTI WITH TUNA AND PANCETTA

Spaghetti alla Carrettiera

½ cup dry porcini mushrooms
1 lb spaghetti
½ cup extra virgin olive oil
2 Tbsp finely chopped garlic
½ lb pancetta, cut in julienne
  strips
6 oz can tuna, drained
Salt
Ground black pepper
½ cup grated Parmesan
  cheese

This is one of my favourite pantry pastas. **Serves 6**

In a small bowl, cover the porcini mushrooms with warm water and soak them for at least 30 minutes until they're soft. Strain the mushrooms through a fine-mesh sieve, reserving the liquid. Pick over the mushrooms, discarding any grit, and chop them roughly.

Bring a large pot of salted water to a boil. Cook the spaghetti until al dente (package directions minus 2 minutes). Drain the spaghetti and set it aside.

While the pasta cooks, heat the olive oil in a large skillet over medium-high heat and sauté the garlic for 1 minute. Add the pancetta and cook for 3 to 4 minutes, or until it's crisp. Stir in the chopped porcini mushrooms and cook for another 3 minutes. Add 3 Tbsp of the reserved porcini soaking liquid, the tuna and salt and freshly ground pepper to taste. Cook for 3 to 4 minutes.

Place the cooked pasta in a warm serving dish, add the sauce and toss together. Garnish with the Parmesan cheese before serving.

SPAGHETTI WITH CLAMS

Spaghetti alle Vongole

1 lb spaghetti

3 lb fresh clams, placed under cold running water for about 5 minutes to remove all sand

½ cup extra virgin olive oil

2 Tbsp finely chopped garlic

4 Roma tomatoes, peeled, seeded, cut in ½-inch dice (1 cup tomato concasse)

Salt

Ground black pepper

½ cup dry white wine

3 Tbsp chopped fresh Italian parsley

This recipe is a feast for the eyes. The tangled spaghetti noodles and plump clams nestled inside their shells, all sprinkled with bright green parsley, look just gorgeous. You can use mussels instead of clams if you prefer. **Serves 6**

Bring a large pot of salted water to a boil. Cook the spaghetti until al dente (package directions minus 2 minutes). Drain the spaghetti and set it aside.

Discard any open clams that do not shut their shell when tapped. Steam the clams in a large pot with 1½ cups boiling salted water until they open. Remove the clams with a slotted spoon and place them in a bowl. Discard any clams that do not open. Remove and discard the shells from half the clams.

Strain the pan juices through a fine-mesh sieve and reserve.

In a skillet over medium heat, heat the olive oil and sweat the garlic for about 2 minutes. Add the tomato concasse and salt and pepper to taste and simmer for 4 minutes. Add the white wine, shelled clams and reserved pan juices and cook for 3 to 4 minutes.

Add the cooked spaghetti and the remaining clams in their shells and stir everything to heat through.

Serve on a large, warm platter and sprinkle with the Italian parsley.

LEFTOVER SPAGHETTI

Spaghetti Avanzati

3 eggs
Salt
Ground black pepper
2 Tbsp Italian parsley
½ lb leftover tomato-based
  spaghetti
1 cup grated Parmesan cheese
¼ cup virgin olive oil

Don't even think about throwing away pasta leftovers. This is a perfect late-night supper or early dinner with the kids. They'll enjoy the idea of spaghetti pizza. This is best served with a simple salad. **Serves 4**

In a stainless steel bowl, whisk together the eggs with salt and pepper to taste and the Italian parsley. Add the spaghetti, freeing up any bits that have stuck together. Let the mixture rest for 10 minutes for the spaghetti to absorb the egg mixture. Mix in the Parmesan cheese.

In a large skillet over medium heat, heat the olive oil for 2 minutes. Add the spaghetti and cook until it's brown, 6 to 8 minutes. Place a lid on the skillet for 3 to 4 minutes to ensure the pasta is heated through. It should look like a frittata with a golden brown bottom.

Invert the pasta onto a serving platter and serve crisp side up.

FETTUCCINE WITH MUSHROOMS

Fettuccine ai Funghi

2 oz dry porcini mushrooms
1 cup lukewarm water
1 lb fettuccine
2 Tbsp butter
1 shallot, finely diced
6 Tbsp Marsala
1 cup vegetable stock
  (page 14)
Pinch saffron, steeped in
  ¼ cup warm water
1 cup whipping cream
¼ cup hazelnuts, roasted,
  skinned, roughly chopped
  (see sidebar page 30)
2 Tbsp chopped Italian parsley
Grated Parmesan cheese
  (optional)

Saffron, cream, Marsala . . . this is one of the richest pantry pastas imaginable. I call it a pantry pasta because it's one you can make with ingredients straight off the shelf. **Serves 6**

In a small bowl, cover the porcini mushrooms with the water and soak them for 20 minutes. Strain them through a fine-mesh sieve, reserving the liquid. Pick over the mushrooms, discarding any grit, and chop them roughly.

Bring a large pot of salted water to a boil. Cook the fettucine until al dente (package directions minus 2 minutes). Drain the fettucine and set it aside.

Heat the butter in a large saucepan on medium-high heat and sauté the shallot and chopped mushrooms for 2 minutes. Add the Marsala and reduce for 2 minutes or by half. Stir in the reserved porcini soaking liquid and the vegetable stock and reduce by half. Add the saffron water and cream and reduce the sauce until it lightly coats the back of a spoon.

Stir the cooked fettuccine into the sauce and mix well until it's heated through. Transfer to a warm pasta bowl and top with the hazelnuts, chopped parsley and Parmesan cheese (if using) to serve.

GLUTTON'S FETTUCCINE
Fettuccine Ghiottone

1 lb fettuccine
2 Tbsp butter
8 oz ground chicken breast
2 Tbsp brandy
2 cups whipping cream
Salt
White pepper
2 Tbsp chopped Italian parsley
6 Tbsp grated Parmesan
  cheese

Our big secret's out now! This isn't usually on the menu at Quattro but our regulars know to request it when they're feeling particularly greedy. Butter, brandy, cream and cheese. What's not to like? Well, maybe your waistline if you enjoy it too often. **Serves 6, or 8 as a starter**

Bring a large pot of salted water to a boil. Cook the fettucine until al dente (package directions minus 2 minutes). Drain the fettucine and set it aside.

Melt the butter in a sauté pan over medium heat. Sauté the chicken for 5 to 6 minutes, breaking it up with a spoon as it cooks. Flambé with the brandy and burn off the alcohol (see sidebar page 160). Add the cream and reduce the sauce until it lightly coats the back of a spoon.

Add the cooked fettuccini and combine it well with the sauce, stirring until the pasta is heated through. Season to taste with salt and white pepper.

Transfer to a large warm pasta bowl and sprinkle with the Italian parsley and Parmesan cheese to serve.

SHRIMP LINGUINE

Linguine con Gamberetti

1 lb linguine
2 Tbsp olive oil
½ lb prawns, peeled, deveined, chopped
4 anchovy fillets, rinsed, dried, chopped
⅓ cup coarsely chopped Italian parsley
2 Tbsp minced garlic
2 Tbsp chopped fresh tarragon
2 tsp lemon zest
2 tsp chili flakes
Pinch of salt
¼ cup Panko breadcrumbs
Cold-press extra virgin olive oil

This is a perfect summer recipe. Anchovies are the secret ingredient in this dish. The other secret is texture. Don't overcook the prawns or pasta. **Serves 6**

Bring a large pot of salted water to a boil. Cook the linguine until al dente (package directions minus 2 minutes). Drain the linguine and set it aside.

Heat the olive oil in a sauté pan over high heat. Add the prawns, anchovies and parsley and cook, stirring, for 30 seconds. Reduce the heat to medium-high and add the garlic, tarragon, lemon zest, chili flakes and pinch of salt. Sauté for 1 minute before adding the cooked pasta. Toss well, slowly adding the breadcrumbs as you do so.

Transfer the pasta into a warm bowl and drizzle with the cold-press extra virgin olive oil.

Save and freeze your prawn shells to make delicious stock or use them in the recipe on page 44.

BEEF AND ARUGULA FUSILLI
Fusilli con Rucola

1 lb beef tenderloin
1 lb fusilli
½ cup extra virgin olive oil
¼ cup finely chopped shallots
1 Tbsp cracked dried chilies
¼ cup finely chopped garlic
1 cup tomato sauce (page 15)
1 cup chopped arugula
8 Roma tomatoes, peeled,
    seeded, cut in ½-inch dice
    (2 cups tomato concasse)
Parmesan cheese for sprinkling
Salt
Ground black pepper

This recipe is a wonderful way to use up leftover beef. Simply slice the cooked beef as thinly as possible and add it to the dish immediately before adding the tomato. If you don't have arugula you can use spinach. **Serves 6**

Freeze the beef for about 1 hour to make it easier to shave with a sharp knife.

Bring a large pot of salted water to a boil. Cook the fusilli until al dente (package directions minus 2 minutes). Drain the fusilli and set it aside.

In a medium to large saucepan, heat the olive oil on medium heat and sauté the shallots, chilies and garlic without browning them. Increase the heat and add the shaved beef tenderloin, tomato sauce and arugula and sauté, stirring, until the beef is barely cooked. Add the tomato and simmer for 3 to 4 minutes. If you're using leftover cooked beef, add it after the tomatoes are cooked.

Toss the pasta with the sauce and add 2 to 3 Tbsp Parmesan cheese and salt and pepper to taste before serving.

BAKED RIGATONI

Timballo di Rigatoni

1 lb rigatoni
½ white onion, finely chopped
2 tsp extra virgin olive oil
2 cups tomato sauce (page 15)
½ cup warm water
Salt
Ground black pepper
1 lb ground pork
½ lb finely diced mortadella
  sausage
1 cup grated Parmesan
  cheese, divided
2 Tbsp chopped Italian parsley
1 egg
All-purpose white flour for
  dusting meatballs
Vegetable oil for frying

This recipe is a great excuse for me to use my favourite deli meat, mortadella. So many pastas are best served immediately, but this one lets you enjoy another glass of wine with your friends while it's in the oven. **Serves 6**

Bring a large pot of salted water to a boil. Cook the rigatoni until al dente (package directions minus 2 minutes). Drain the rigatoni and set it aside.

Sauté the onion in the olive oil over medium heat for 3 to 4 minutes, or until it's translucent. Add the tomato sauce, warm water and salt and pepper to taste. Reduce the heat to low and cook for 15 minutes.

Preheat the oven to 375°F.

Combine the pork, mortadella, half the Parmesan cheese, the parsley and the egg. Form the mixture into small meatballs and roll in the flour.

Heat a thin film of the vegetable oil in a skillet over medium-high heat. Shake the pan to brown the meatballs on all surfaces. Transfer the meatballs with a slotted spoon to the tomato sauce and cook for 7 to 8 minutes on low heat. Add the partially cooked pasta and mix everything together. Spoon the pasta and sauce into a baking dish, sprinkle with the remaining Parmesan and bake for 15 to 20 minutes, or until the rigatoni is heated through.

SPICY PENNE
Penne Arrabiata

2 oz lardo (*strutto*) or
   European-style bacon, cut
   in ½-inch dice
1 onion, cut in ½-inch dice
2 Tbsp finely minced garlic
½ lb pancetta, julienned
One 28 oz can tomatoes,
   seeds removed (see sidebar)
1 lb penne (penne rigate
   holds sauce best)
1 Tbsp peperoncino
Salt
½ cup grated pecorino
   Romano

Arrabiata means "upset" or "angry" in Italian, but I guarantee that you won't be when you taste this simple pasta dish. **Serves 6**

In a skillet on high heat, fry the lardo with the onion and garlic, stirring, for about 3 minutes. Add the pancetta and cook, stirring, until the pancetta is crisp. Add the tomatoes, reduce the heat to medium and cook for 10 minutes.

While the tomatoes cook, bring a large pot of salted water to a boil. Cook the penne until al dente (package directions minus 2 minutes). Drain the penne and set it aside.

Add the peperoncino to the sauce. Season to taste with salt. Toss the pasta with the sauce and heat through.

Garnish with pecorino Romano to serve in a warm pasta or serving bowl.

To remove seeds from canned tomatoes, put them through a food mill with a fine disk or push through a sieve with a wooden spoon. Canned *plum* tomatoes, preferably from Italy, have more substance, less juice and less acidity.

PENNE WITH CURRIED APPLES

Penne Melate

1 Tbsp extra virgin olive oil
2 shallots, finely diced
1½ lb chicken breast,
   boneless, skinless, cut in
   ¾-inch cubes
2 cups dry white wine
2 Tbsp curry powder diluted
   in ½ cup water
1 lb penne rigate
2 Granny Smith apples,
   peeled, cored, cut in
   ½-inch dice
2 Tbsp finely chopped Italian
   parsley

You may be surprised to learn that we use a lot of curry powder in Italy. Any short pasta would work well with this recipe. **Serves 6**

Heat a 10-inch sauté pan over medium heat and add the olive oil. Sauté the shallots until they've softened, about 2 minutes. Increase the heat to medium-high, add the chicken and sauté for 2 minutes. Stir in the white wine and reduce it for 5 minutes, or until it's nearly dry. Add the curry water, cover and cook for 10 minutes.

Meanwhile, bring a large pot of salted water to a boil. Cook the penne until al dente (package directions minus 2 minutes). Drain the penne and set it aside.

Add the apples to the sauce and cook for 4 minutes. Stir in the cooked pasta, tossing it to coat it with the sauce and heat it through.

Pour the pasta into a warm pasta serving bowl and sprinkle the parsley overtop to serve.

PENNE WITH MASCARPONE AND ITALIAN SAUSAGE

Penne di Mia Sorella

1 lb penne rigate
4 pieces Italian sausage, about
   4 oz each, skin removed and
   chopped finely
½ cup extra virgin olive oil
8 oz tub mascarpone
¼ cup grated Parmigiano
   Reggiano
Heavy cracked black pepper
   straight from mill
3 Tbsp Italian parsley

Years ago my sister used to make this for me all the time. I miss those days. Luckily this recipe is fast and easy, but you have to eat it the moment it comes out of the skillet. If it cools even a little you lose a lot of the flavour. **Serves 6**

Bring a large pot of salted water to a boil. Cook the penne until al dente (package directions minus 2 minutes). Drain the penne and set it aside.

In a large skillet over medium heat, sauté the sausage in the extra virgin olive oil for 6 to 8 minutes, or until cooked. Add the penne and remove the pan from the heat.

Mix in the mascarpone, Parmesan and cracked black pepper until the mascarpone coats the penne evenly.

Sprinkle with parsley and serve in warm bowls.

SPINACH RAVIOLINI WITH TRUFFLE OIL

Raviolini ai Spinaci

1½ cups all-purpose white
    flour
6 egg yolks
4 oz fresh spinach, washed,
    stems removed, steamed,
    drained then puréed (makes
    ⅓ cup)
1 egg for egg wash
1 Tbsp water
½ cup mashed potatoes,
    mixed with salt, ground
    black pepper and 1 Tbsp
    hot milk to make them soft
8 quail eggs, boiled for 5
    minutes, cooled in cold
    water and shells removed
2 Tbsp white truffle oil
1 tsp chopped fresh sage
¼ cup butter

This is an aspiration recipe. When I was growing up this pasta was commonly served at very extravagant weddings. Today you can buy quail eggs in any specialty store, making this dish accessible but still special. (This recipe may be served on its own or with Open-Faced Scallop and Apple Lasagna (page 98) for a really beautiful presentation.) **Makes 16 raviolini, serves 4 or more as a starter**

For the pasta, place the flour in the bowl of a stand mixer fitted with a dough hook.

In a separate bowl, whisk together the egg yolks and puréed spinach. With the stand mixer on low speed, slowly add this egg mixture to the flour and mix until a solid ball forms. The dough should be firm but soft to the touch. Wrap the dough in plastic wrap and let it rest for at least 1 hour, or overnight.

Make an egg wash by beating the egg with the water.

Roll the dough through a pasta machine on its thinnest setting, or by hand with a rolling pin, to create 2 long rectangles of pasta. Spoon out 16 portions of mashed potato onto 1 of the pasta sheets. Place in even rows of 2 × 8 and lightly brush the egg wash between and around all the pillows of filling.

Slice the quail eggs in half lengthwise and place 1 half on top of each mashed potato filling. Sprinkle with the truffle oil and place the second sheet of pasta on top. Use your finger to press down around each raviolini. Cut the pasta into 16 raviolini and pinch the borders tightly to seal them securely.

Bring a large pot of salted water to a boil. Place the raviolini in the rapidly boiling water and cook until the pasta floats to the top, 4 to 5 minutes.

Meanwhile, sauté the sage in the butter.

Remove the pasta from water with a slotted spoon and arrange in warm pasta bowls. Drizzle with the sage butter and serve hot.

BUTTERNUT SQUASH RAVIOLI

Ravioli Zuccati

RAVIOLI

1 small butternut squash
  (1½–2 lb)
2 tsp olive oil
1 bay leaf
1 Tbsp black truffle paste
½ cup grated Parmesan
  cheese
½ tsp salt
Pinch ground black pepper
½ cup fresh breadcrumbs
1 recipe basic pasta dough
  (page 20)

SAUCE

½ lb butter
1 clove garlic, finely chopped
1 Tbsp finely chopped fresh
  sage
½ cup chopped toasted
  walnuts
Salt
Ground black pepper

Go ahead and spoil yourself with this. It's so rich and round and buttery that you'll still be fantasizing about it after the last piece has been devoured. **Serves 6**

Preheat the oven to 375°F. Line a baking sheet with parchment paper.

Cut the squash in half lengthwise, remove the seeds and brush the cut surfaces with the olive oil. Place ½ bay leaf on each half.

Place the cut side down on the prepared baking sheet and roast it for about 40 minutes, or until the flesh is soft. Cool, then scoop out and purée the flesh. Let cool completely.

In a bowl, combine the squash purée, truffle paste, Parmesan cheese, salt and pepper. Add the breadcrumbs as needed to make a mixture that holds its shape when scooped with a spoon.

Roll the pasta dough through a pasta machine, or by hand with a rolling pin, into large sheets. Cut the pasta into 4-inch squares.

If you have a ravioli board, use it to stuff the pasta with squash filling. Alternatively, spoon mounds of filling onto 1 square, brush water on a second square and place this, wet side down, over the filling. Press gently around the filling with your fingers to seal all the edges. Repeat until you have used all the filling.

Cook the ravioli in plenty of rapidly boiling, salted water for 2 to 3 minutes. Drain and reserve.

Meanwhile, make the sauce. Melt the butter in a saucepan, add the chopped garlic and sauté for 1 minute. Add the sage and walnuts. Season to taste with salt and pepper. Toss with the ravioli and serve immediately in warm pasta bowls.

TRUFFLE AND MUSHROOM RAVIOLI

Ravioli Piemontesi

RAVIOLI

2 oz fresh chanterelle
   mushrooms, cut in small
   dice
2 oz portobello mushrooms,
   cut in small dice
2 Tbsp white truffle oil
¼ tsp chopped fresh sage
½ cup mascarpone
½ cup ricotta
½ cup grated Parmesan
   cheese
1 recipe basic pasta dough
   (page 20)
Flour for dusting

SAUCE

¾ cup hot water
½ cup dry porcini mushrooms
1 cup whipping cream
2 Tbsp white truffle oil
½ tsp chopped fresh sage
Salt
Ground black pepper

EGG WASH

1 egg
1 Tbsp water

This recipe is perfect as an appetizer or a vegetarian main course. It's very earthy and lusty, and packs a punch like no other meatless dish I've tried. This is one of Quattro's tried and true recipes. **Serves 6**

For the filling, heat a large sauté pan over medium-high heat. Sauté the chanterelle and portobello mushrooms in the truffle oil and sage until they've softened and have absorbed all their juices. Remove from the heat and let cool. When cool, combine the mushrooms with the 3 cheeses in a large bowl.

For the sauce, pour the hot water over the dry porcini mushrooms, cover and steep for 30 minutes, or until softened. Strain the mushrooms through a fine-mesh sieve or cheesecloth, and reserve the liquid. Inspect the mushrooms, discarding any grit, and chop them finely.

Mix the chopped porcini mushrooms and their reserved soaking liquid, whipping cream, truffle oil, sage and a little salt and pepper in a saucepan over medium heat. Reduce the sauce to thicken it.

Make an egg wash by beating the egg with the water in a small bowl.

Lightly dust a rimmed cookie sheet with semolina or all-purpose white flour.

Lay a pasta sheet over a floured ravioli board, or roll out 2 strips of pasta, and brush with the egg wash. Place a spoonful of mushroom-cheese filling in each indented space. Cover with a second sheet of pasta and run a rolling pin over the top to seal the filling in the pockets. Separate the pieces with a small knife and place in a single layer on the prepared cookie sheet, covered loosely with a tea towel. Repeat with the remaining filling and pasta.

Bring a large pan of salted water to a boil. Drop the ravioli in for about 3 minutes. Drain.

Serve on warm plates and drizzle with the sauce.

OPEN-FACED SCALLOP AND APPLE LASAGNA

Lasagnetta Ventaglio

SAFFRON PASTA

⅓ cup semolina flour + extra
    for dusting
1 cup all-purpose white flour
9 large egg yolks
1 tsp olive oil
Pinch saffron

SPINACH PASTA

1½ cups + 1 tsp all-purpose
    white flour
6 large egg yolks
⅓ cup spinach purée
    (page 95)

SCALLOP AND APPLE FILLING

1 tsp butter
2 Fuji apples, peeled, cored,
    sliced
1 shallot, diced
Salt
Ground black pepper
16 large Alaskan scallops

SAUCE

¼ cup butter
4 fresh tomatoes, peeled,
    seeded, diced
2 Tbsp chopped Italian parsley

This free-form lasagna is a triple treat. It's beautiful to look at, delicious to eat and simple to prepare. You can serve it alone but it's also very good alongside Spinach Raviolini with Truffle Oil (page 95). You can also use plain pasta dough for this recipe if you prefer.

Serves 8

Dust a baking tray with semolina flour.

For the saffron pasta, add the flours to the bowl of a stand mixer fitted with a dough hook. In a separate bowl, whisk together the egg yolks, oil and saffron. Add this to the flour and mix until a solid ball forms. The dough should be firm but soft to the touch.

For the spinach pasta, add the flour to the bowl of a stand mixer fitted with a dough hook. In a separate bowl, whisk together the egg yolks and spinach purée. Add this to the flour and mix until a solid ball forms. The dough should be firm but soft to the touch.

Flatten each portion of dough with your hands and wrap them separately in plastic wrap. Set the doughs aside to rest for at least 1 hour.

For the saffron pasta, divide the dough into 2 pieces. While you work with the saffron pasta, keep the spinach pasta covered with a damp towel. Working with 1 sheet at a time, feed the saffron dough through a pasta machine set to its thinnest setting, or use a rolling pin to roll the pasta out by hand. Cut the saffron sheets into four 4-inch squares to give you 8 squares of saffron pasta.

Repeat with the spinach pasta, again making 8 squares of pasta.

Place all the pasta squares on the prepared tray and cover them lightly with a kitchen towel until you're ready to cook.

Cook the pasta in plenty of rapidly boiling, salted water for 2 to 3 minutes. Drain.

For the filling, melt the butter and sauté the sliced apples and shallot, seasoning to taste with salt and pepper. Season the scallops with more salt and pepper then slice half of them horizontally into 4 coins. Set the apple mixture and scallops aside.

For the sauce, melt the butter and sauté the tomatoes on low heat until they're heated through. Keep them warm.

(continued on page 100)

OPEN-FACED SCALLOP AND APPLE LASAGNA (CONT'D)

Preheat the oven to 325°F. Line a baking sheet with parchment paper. (You may need 2 sheets.)

Place 8 spinach pasta squares on the prepared baking sheet. Spoon apple mixture in the centre of each square and place 4 slices of scallop on top of each pile. Lay a saffron pasta square on top of the scallop slices, angled so that the spinach pasta shows. Cover with tinfoil and bake for 5 to 8 minutes.

Meanwhile, grill or sauté the remaining whole scallops for about 2 minutes on each side.

Remove the lasagnetta from the oven and carefully transfer them to warm serving plates. Spoon the tomato butter sauce overtop and sprinkle them with the Italian parsley. Place a grilled scallop on top of each lasagnetta.

If you're serving this with Spinach Raviolini, place 4 raviolini around the lasagnetta to form a square.

AMATRICIANA BUCATINI

Bucatini all' Amatriciana

1 lb package bucatini
½ cup extra virgin olive oil
½ lb smoked *guanciale*, cut
   in julienne strips
¼ lb pancetta, cut in julienne
   strips
2 Tbsp red wine vinegar
4 Roma tomatoes, peeled,
   seeded, cut in ½-inch dice
   (1 cup tomato concasse)
1 Tbsp tomato paste
1 Tbsp peperoncino
2 Tbsp fresh basil leaves
¼ cup grated pecorino
   Romano

Don't be shy about tying your napkin around your neck for this one. Bucatini—thick, tubular spaghetti noodles—are meant for slurping. *Guanciale* is bacon prepared from pig's cheek—but don't let that put you off! **Serves 6**

Bring a large pot of salted water to a boil. Cook the bucatini until al dente (package directions minus 2 minutes). Drain the bucatini and set it aside.

Heat the olive oil in a large sauté pan on medium heat. Fry the guanciale and pancetta until they're crisp. Add the red wine vinegar and reduce for 1 minute, by about half. Add the tomato concasse, tomato paste and peperoncino, stirring to mix well, and cook for 5 minutes.

Tear the fresh basil roughly and stir it into the sauce. Add the cooked bucatini and stir until it's heated through and well mixed with the sauce. Toss with the pecorino Romano and serve immediately.

You shouldn't need to add salt or pepper to this dish.

BRAISED RABBIT CANNELLONI
Cannelloni al Coniglio

BÉCHAMEL SAUCE

1¾ cups whole milk (room temperature)
¼ cup butter
¼ cup all-purpose white flour
¾ tsp salt
¼ tsp ground black pepper
1 recipe saffron pasta (page 98)

RABBIT FILLING

2½–3 lb rabbit
Salt
Ground black pepper
2 Tbsp vegetable oil, divided
2 stalks celery, cut in small dice
1 carrot, cut in small dice
1 onion, cut in small dice
4 cups hot chicken stock (page 10)
Bouquet garni: 1 bay leaf, 12 black peppercorns and 2 sprigs thyme tied in cheesecloth
4 oz fresh chanterelle mushrooms
¼ cup pitted and chopped Taggiasche olives (avoid using salty cured olives for this recipe)
¼ cup grated Parmesan cheese
1 tsp fennel seeds

My uncle used to keep rabbits, so it was always on the table when I was growing up. I developed this recipe for our very popular Postcards from Italy promotion. This rustic rabbit dish is by far my favourite cannelloni recipe. Just don't tell the children what's in it. **Serves 6**

For the béchamel sauce, heat the milk in a saucepan on medium heat until it comes to a boil.

In another saucepan, melt the butter on medium-low heat. Remove from the heat and whisk in the flour. Return to the heat and cook for 1 minute. Add the hot milk all at once and whisk constantly until the mixture is smooth and thick and returns to a boil. Remove the sauce from the heat and stir in the salt and pepper.

Scrape the sauce into a bowl. Cover it with a piece of plastic wrap pressed right against the surface to prevent a skin from forming. Refrigerate it until it's needed.

Lightly dust a rimmed cookie sheet with semolina or all-purpose white flour.

Wrap the saffron pasta dough in plastic wrap and let sit for at least 1 hour, or up to 1 day in the fridge. Roll the dough through a pasta machine, finishing with the thinnest setting, or use a rolling pin to roll it out to a thickness of ⅛ inch. Use a sharp knife to cut the pasta into 4-inch squares. Transfer them to the prepared cookie sheet, making sure not to overlap the squares. Cover the cookie sheet loosely with a tea towel and keep at room temperature until you're ready to cook the pasta.

Cook the pasta in plenty of rapidly boiling, salted water for 2 to 3 minutes, until al dente. Drain it, then place it in a clean container and cover it with cold water until you're ready to fill it.

Preheat the oven to 325°F.

Cut the rabbit into quarters and season it with salt and pepper. Heat 1 Tbsp of the oil in a skillet on medium-high heat. Sear the rabbit for 2 to 3 minutes per side, until it's browned. Transfer the rabbit to a shallow ovenproof pan.

Add the celery, carrot and onion to the skillet on medium heat and sauté for about 5 minutes, stirring often, until the vegetables soften. Add the sautéed vegetables to the rabbit and cover with the hot chicken stock. Add the bouquet garni, cover the pan with a lid and braise in the oven for about 3 hours. If the liquid boils rapidly, reduce the heat. The rabbit is cooked when the meat is tender and nearly falling off the bones.

SALSA VELLUTATA
2 Tbsp butter
2 Tbsp all-purpose white flour
½ cup chopped tomato
1 tsp chopped fresh oregano
1 tsp chopped fresh tarragon

½ cup grated Parmesan
    cheese for garnish

Remove the pan from the oven and let the rabbit cool in the pan juices. When the rabbit's cool, transfer it to a cutting board, reserving the pan juices. Remove and discard all the bones. Work carefully because there are many tiny ones. Shred the rabbit meat and place it in a bowl.

Strain the pan juices through a fine-mesh sieve into a clean bowl.

Heat the remaining oil in a skillet on medium-high heat. Sauté the chanterelles for 5 minutes, until golden brown. Add to the rabbit meat. Mix in the olives, Parmesan cheese, fennel seeds and enough béchamel to bind the filling.

For the salsa vellutata, melt the butter in a saucepan on medium-low heat. Remove the pan from the heat and stir in the flour. Return to the heat and cook for 1 minute. Whisk in the pan juices strained from the rabbit. Bring the sauce to a simmer and cook for about 20 minutes, until it's reduced by one-third. Stir in the tomato, oregano and tarragon.

Preheat the oven to 350°F.

Drain and pat dry the pasta squares. Lay them out on a lightly floured surface. Place 2 Tbsp of the rabbit filling along the bottom edge of each square, then roll up to make cannelloni.

Spoon a thin layer of salsa vellutata into the bottom of a shallow baking dish big enough to hold all the cannelloni in 1 layer. Place the cannelloni, seam side down, in the dish, cover them with the remaining salsa and bake for about 15 minutes, until heated through.

Place 2 or 3 cannelloni on warm plates and garnish with the Parmesan cheese.

CHICKEN ROTOLO
Rotolo Farcito

2 Tbsp butter

½ lb ground chicken

2 Tbsp brandy

2 lb ricotta

½ cup cooked, drained, squeezed of excess water and chopped spinach

2 egg yolks

1 whole egg

½ cup grated Parmesan cheese

Pinch nutmeg

Salt

Ground black pepper

4 large pasta sheets (10 × 10 inches) (page 20)*

3 cups hot tomato sauce (page 15)

3 cups hot cream sauce (page 16)

2 Tbsp finely chopped Italian parsley

* You can also use prepared fresh pasta sheets, pre-cooked about 3 minutes in salted boiling water to make them easier to work with. They swell slightly and may be cut in 10-inch squares.

I hadn't been in Canada for more than a month when my Italian driving habits landed me in some hot water. What a great start! My brother's friend helped me out in a big way and to say thank you, Edith and I invited the friend and the only other couples we knew over for dinner. Eager to impress our new friends I made this dish, and everyone wanted to take home the leftovers. Serve this pasta the next time you want to make friends or say thank you. **Makes 4 rotolo, serves 6**

Heat the butter in a sauté pan over medium heat and cook the chicken for 3 minutes. Flambé with the brandy and let cool (see sidebar page 160).

In a mixing bowl, combine the cooked chicken with the ricotta, spinach, egg yolks and egg, Parmesan cheese, nutmeg and salt and pepper to taste.

On a clean work surface, lay out a 12- × 12-inch double-thickness piece of cheesecloth, top it with lightly oiled waxed paper and centre 1 pasta sheet on top.

Spread one-quarter of the filling mixture over the pasta sheet to within 1 inch of the top edge. Brush the pasta on its top edge with water. Roll the filled pasta away from you. The water will act like glue and stick the pasta together. Wrap the pasta roll in the parchment paper, twist the ends together, wrap in the cheesecloth and tie the ends tightly with kitchen string. Repeat process for the remaining 3 rolls. Cook in boiling water for 30 minutes.

Remove the rolls from the water and let cool slightly to allow the filling to set. Remove the cheesecloth and waxed paper and slice into 1½-inch-thick pieces to serve.

Arrange 4 slices on each plate, topping 2 of the slices with ¼ cup of the hot tomato sauce and the remaining 2 slices with ¼ cup hot cream sauce.

Garnish with chopped Italian parsley and serve.

SEAFOOD RISOTTO

Risotto Pescatore

6 Tbsp salted butter, divided
½ onion, diced
1 lb scallops, cut in half if large
1 cup dry white wine
Pinch saffron
2 cups arborio rice
3 cups fish stock (page 12), kept hot
1 lb hand-peeled baby shrimp
Salt
Ground black pepper
2 Tbsp chopped fresh dill
1 Tbsp chopped chives

This is a classic seafood risotto recipe. If you're looking for something extra, top it with one of the clam or mussel dishes (pages 134 to 138). **Serves 6–8**

Heat half the butter in a heavy-bottomed saucepan over medium heat. Sauté the onion for 3 minutes, stirring. Add the scallops and sauté for 2 minutes. Remove the scallops from the pan and reserve. Do not remove the onions.

Deglaze the pan with the white wine, add the pinch of saffron and cook for 3 minutes. Add the rice and stir for 1 minute. Add 1½ cups of the hot fish stock, stirring constantly and gently. Continue to stir, adding the remaining stock as necessary to cook the rice al dente. You may not need all the stock. Do not allow the pan to become dry on the bottom. Fold in the baby shrimp and sautéed scallops and heat through. Season to taste with salt and pepper.

Remove the risotto from the heat and add the fresh dill, chives and remaining butter. Ladle it into warm bowls to serve.

PEA AND PROSCIUTTO RISOTTO

Risotto con Piselli e Prosciutto

12 slices prosciutto, cut in
   julienne strips
1 Tbsp extra virgin olive oil
1 shallot, finely diced
½ onion, diced
1 Tbsp finely chopped garlic
2 cups arborio rice
8 cups chicken stock
   (page 10), kept hot
1 cup sweet peas, frozen
   if fresh are not available
Salt
Ground black pepper
6 Tbsp salted butter
⅓ cup grated Parmesan
   cheese

This recipe makes me think of Venice. I ordered it whenever I went out for dinner when I was working there in my teens. You could call it my "pink and green" period. The colours make this a particularly pretty dish. **Serves 6**

In a heavy saucepan, sauté the prosciutto in the extra virgin olive oil for 4 to 5 minutes over medium-high heat until it starts to crisp.

Add the shallot, onion and garlic to the prosciutto and sauté for 1 minute, stirring to prevent burning. Add the rice and stir for 2 minutes until all the grains of rice are coated with oil. Add half the hot chicken stock and stir occasionally to prevent the rice from sticking.

As the rice absorbs the stock, slowly stir in more liquid, 1 ladle at a time, never allowing the bottom of the pan to dry out. You may not need all the stock. Once the rice has been added you should allow 15 to 18 minutes of cooking time. Bite into the rice toward the end of the cooking time to test its doneness. When the rice is just about al dente, fold in the peas and continue cooking until they're hot and the rice is just cooked and creamy.

Season to taste with salt and pepper. Remove the risotto from the heat and stir in the butter and Parmesan cheese.

Serve hot.

ITALIAN SAUSAGE RISOTTO

Risotto con Salsicce

2 oz dry porcini mushrooms,
  soaked in 4 cups warm water
  about 1 hour
¼ cup butter, divided
½ white onion, diced
4 mild Italian sausages, skin
  removed, chopped
1 cup dry red wine
2 cups arborio rice
12 cups chicken stock
  (page 10), kept hot
¼ cup grated Parmesan
  cheese
Salt
Ground black pepper

Some risottos are very delicate and velvety. This one isn't! **Serves 6**

Strain the porcini mushrooms through a fine-mesh sieve, reserving the liquid. Pick through the mushrooms, discarding any grit, and then chop them.

Over medium heat in a heavy sauté pan, melt 2 Tbsp of the butter and sauté the onion for 2 minutes. Add the sausage and chopped porcini mushrooms and sauté for 5 minutes. Deglaze the pan with the red wine and reduce for 2 minutes. Stir in the rice and cook for 1 to 2 minutes until the rice is coated with pan juices and is heated through.

Increase the heat to medium-high and slowly add half the hot chicken stock and half the reserved mushroom liquid, stirring gently and constantly. Add more liquid if required. You may not need all the liquid as the rice should be al dente but not chalky or mushy.

Remove the risotto from the heat and melt in the remaining butter and the Parmesan cheese. Season to taste with salt and pepper.

Serve in warm bowls.

RISOTTO BALLS | *Suppli*

When I was a young boy growing up just outside Rome, there were as many *tavola calda* as there are Starbucks in Vancouver today. My favourite street-vendor snack was *suppli*, basically plain risotto balls with mozzarella and tomato sauce. Here are two of my favourite *suppli* recipes.

BEEF AND PORCINI MUSHROOMS RISOTTO BALLS
Arancini di Riso

Makes 24 pieces

4 cups cooked risotto (page 21) with a pinch of saffron added
½ cup grated pecorino Romano
½ onion, finely diced
2 Tbsp olive oil
1 lb ground beef
3 fresh sage leaves
2 stalks celery, finely diced
1 oz dried porcini mushroom, soaked in lukewarm water and chopped
6 Tbsp dry white wine
2 Tbsp tomato paste
Salt
Ground black pepper
1 cup frozen green peas
½ lb caciocavallo, cut into ½-inch cubes
¼ cup all-purpose white flour
4 eggs, lightly beaten
2 cups fresh breadcrumbs
Vegetable oil for frying

Allow the saffron risotto to cool then add the pecorino Romano. Let cool.

Preheat the oven to 350°F.

In a sauté pan over medium heat, sauté the onion in the olive oil for about 2 minutes. Add the beef, sage, celery and porcini mushrooms and brown the beef. Add the white wine, tomato paste and salt and pepper to taste.

Cook until the liquid evaporates. Cool then add the peas.

Place about 2 Tbsp of saffron risotto in the palm of your hand. Press some beef mixture into the centre, add 1 cube of caciocavallo cheese and form a ball around the beef and cheese with the risotto. Roll the ball in the flour, then the beaten egg, then the breadcrumbs.

Repeat with the remaining rice; you should get about 24 risotto balls.

Over medium-high heat in an ovenproof skillet, brown the balls evenly in the vegetable oil then bake them for 10 minutes, or until the internal temperature melts the cheese.

Serve on a large platter.

LAMB SAUSAGE AND ASIAGO CHEESE RISOTTO BALLS
Suppli al Pascolo

2 Tbsp unsalted butter
1 shallot, finely diced
10 oz lamb sausage, casing removed, crumbled
2 cups arborio rice
¼ cup dry white wine
8 cups chicken stock (page 10), kept hot
1 bay leaf
¾ cup grated Parmesan cheese
Salt
2 oz Asiago cheese, cut into eighteen ½-inch cubes
All-purpose white flour for coating
3 cups Panko breadcrumbs
3 eggs, beaten

Makes 18 pieces

Melt the butter in a large sauté pan over medium heat and sweat the shallot for 1 minute. Add the sausage and cook for 3 minutes, breaking it up into smaller pieces as it cooks. Stir in the rice, increase the heat to medium-high and stir for 1 minute until the rice is coated with butter. Add the wine and half the hot stock. Stir for about 7 minutes, making sure the rice does not stick to bottom of pan. Add the bay leaf.

Gradually ladle in the remaining hot stock, stirring until the rice is cooked al dente, about 12 minutes.

Stir in the Parmesan cheese. Season to taste with salt if necessary. Spread out on a rimmed baking sheet to cool.

This recipe makes twice as much risotto as you need for the risotto balls. Refrigerate the unused portion and reheat it within 3 days.

Preheat the oven to 400°F and position a rack in the centre. If you have a deep fryer, fill it with vegetable oil and preheat it to 375°F; alternatively fill a large deep-sided sauté pan halfway with vegetable oil and heat it to 375°F. Remember safety in the kitchen: turn the handle away from the edge of the stovetop.

Form the risotto into eighteen 2-inch balls. Poke a hole in the centre of each and insert an Asiago cube.

Place the flour and Panko crumbs in separate dishes, with the bowl of beaten eggs beside them. Dust 1 ball lightly in flour then dip it in egg, roll it in Panko crumbs, dip it in egg again and then in the Panko crumbs again.

Deep-fry or shallow-fry the risotto balls in the hot oil until they're golden brown. Transfer them to a rimmed baking sheet and bake them for about 10 minutes, until the cheese has melted inside.

These are great served at room temperature. If you make them smaller you can serve them with cocktails. You can use any risotto recipe, and you could substitute chorizo for lamb sausage if you prefer.

SEARED POLENTA

Polenta in Padella

2 tsp olive oil
1 small onion, finely diced
3 cloves garlic, finely chopped
6 cups water
½ tsp salt
1½ cups cornmeal
½ cup mascarpone cheese
⅓ cup grated Parmesan cheese
½ cup unsalted butter, cubed and kept cold
2 sprigs thyme, leaves only, chopped
White pepper
1 Tbsp canola oil for sautéing

This is a rich and versatile version of an Italian staple. Polenta is great food for children. You can cut it into fun shapes or have Italian-style french fries. Just don't dip them in ketchup! **Serves 8**

In a heavy saucepan, heat the olive oil and sauté the onion until translucent but not browned. Stir in the garlic and cook for 2 minutes. Add the water and salt and bring to a boil. Reduce the heat to medium and gradually whisk in the cornmeal.

Over medium heat, continue to whisk once all the cornmeal has been added as it thickens quickly. When the mixture is thick, turn off the heat. Add the cheeses, butter, thyme and pepper to taste, and whisk well to combine. Pour the polenta into a 9- × 13-inch glass dish. Chill, covered, for at least 6 hours to set.

Once the polenta has set, cut it into your preferred shape: circles, squares, triangles, etc.

Preheat the oven to 400°F.

In a non-stick ovenproof pan, heat the canola oil over medium-high heat. Sear the polenta on one side. Transfer the pan to the oven and bake for 5 to 7 minutes. Carefully remove the polenta from the pan and flip it over.

Serve the polenta warm, seared side up.

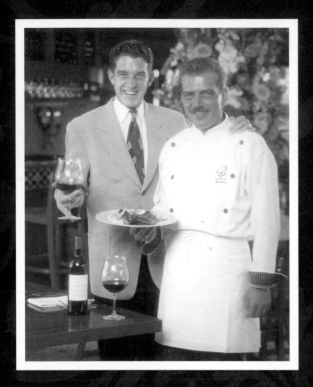

SEAFOOD
Frutti di Mare

SALMON FILLET WITH HONEY
Salmone al Miele

2 cups freshly squeezed
   orange juice reduced to
   ¼ cup
¼ cup grainy Dijon mustard
2 Tbsp chopped fresh dill
½ cup wildflower or other
   liquid honey
3 lb boneless wild salmon
   fillet, skin on or off
Salt
Ground black pepper

I make this on the barbecue all the time in summer. It's so easy and fast. You can prepare it in advance and then just pop it on the grill when your guests arrive. Sometimes I serve it as an appetizer and just put it right on the table and open the foil. Talk about family-style. *Mangia, mangia!* **Serves 6–8**

Preheat the oven or barbecue to 400°F.

Combine the reduced orange juice, grainy Dijon, dill and honey.

Place the salmon on a large sheet of lightly oiled aluminum foil, skin side down. Season the salmon with salt and pepper and spread the glaze on top. Seal the foil and place it on a rimmed baking pan in the oven, or if using the barbecue, place the foil packet directly on the grill. Bake for 8 to 9 minutes for each inch of thickness, or until the salmon is cooked. Open the foil to see if the salmon is cooked to your liking. Let it rest for 5 minutes.

Transfer the salmon from the foil to a large platter and spoon over the cooking juices.

If you prefer a crusty glaze on your salmon, you can cook it on a foil-lined baking sheet instead of enclosing it in foil.

SALMON FILLET WITH FENNEL
Salmone Finocchiato

SALMON

1 Tbsp chopped fresh tarragon
1 Tbsp extra virgin olive oil
1 tsp peperoncino
6 fillets wild salmon (about
   6 oz each)
Salt
Ground black pepper

CARAMELIZED ONIONS

2 medium onions cut in thin
   julienne strips
1 tsp butter
1 Tbsp granulated sugar

SAUCE

1 Tbsp butter
2 bulbs fennel, cores removed,
   cut in thin julienne strips
1 shallot, finely chopped
1 cup Sauvignon Blanc, or
   other similar white wine
2 cups whipping cream
Salt
Ground black pepper

Serve this dish with simple boiled potatoes tossed with olive oil and parsley. The caramelized onions add a nice sweetness to the salmon, and they're perfect the next day with Italian sausage, so make some extra. **Serves 6**

Combine the tarragon, olive oil and peperoncino in a small bowl and rub over the salmon flesh. Marinate the salmon for 1 hour at room temperature.

For the caramelized onions, cook the onions and butter in a large sauté pan over low heat until the onions are very soft and translucent. After 20 minutes, sprinkle the onions with the sugar and continue cooking, stirring frequently to prevent burning, until they're a rich brown.

While the onions caramelize, make the sauce. Heat the butter in a saucepan over medium heat and sweat the fennel and shallot for 4 minutes, or until they've softened. Add the wine and reduce until almost dry. Stir in the whipping cream and reduce further until the sauce coats the back of a spoon. Season to taste with salt and pepper.

Preheat the oven to 400°F.

Heat an ovenproof skillet on medium heat. Season the salmon with salt and pepper and sear for 3 minutes on each side. Finish cooking it in the oven for 3 to 4 minutes, or until it's cooked to your taste. The cooking time will depend on the thickness of the salmon fillets.

Place the fennel sauce on a warm platter and arrange the fish on top. Scatter caramelized onions over the fish.

LIMONCELLO ORANGE ROUGHY

Roughy di Arancia con Limoncello

Six 6 oz portions orange roughy
Salt
Ground black pepper
2 tsp olive oil
1 Tbsp chopped tarragon
1 Tbsp chopped fresh basil
1 Tbsp chopped parsley
1 Tbsp chopped chives
2 Tbsp canola oil
2 cups fish stock (page 12)
1 bulb fennel, sliced very thinly
   using a mandolin
⅔ cup Limoncello
1 bunch rapini, blanched in
   boiling water for 1 minute,
   drained well
1 Tbsp extra virgin olive oil
1 Tbsp chopped garlic
Pinch chili flakes

This dish was inspired by a meal I had in Positano on the Amalfi Coast. We went to a little restaurant and had a simple grilled fish fresh from the sea. That dish was followed by an icy cold glass of Limoncello. I still had the flavour of the fish in my mouth and it tasted great. I thought, wow, why don't we combine them together in one recipe. So I did, and now you can, too. **Serves 6**

Season the orange roughy with salt, pepper and olive oil. Place the tarragon, basil, parsley and chives on the top of the roughy.

Preheat the oven to 400°F.

Heat the canola oil in an ovenproof skillet on medium-high heat, add the orange roughy herb side down and sear on that side only. Flip the fish, transfer the skillet to the oven and roast for 6½ minutes.

In a saucepan over medium-high heat, bring the fish stock and fennel to a boil. Lower the heat and simmer to reduce by half. Season to taste with more salt and pepper and add the Limoncello. Simmer until you're ready to serve.

Sauté the rapini in the extra virgin olive oil with the garlic, chili flakes and more salt and pepper until softened.

Place the sautéed rapini in a bowl and top it with the cooked orange roughy. Pour Limoncello reduction overtop and serve.

BAKED LONG LINE LING COD WITH FENNEL
Merluzzo al Cartoccio

12 cherry tomatoes, halved
1 red onion, cut in thin
    julienne strips
1 bulb fennel, cut in thin
    julienne strips
1 Tbsp finely chopped garlic
Six 6 oz fillets fresh ling cod
¾ cup Pinot Grigio or other
    fruity white wine
1 Tbsp finely chopped Italian
    parsley
1 Tbsp fennel fronds or
    chopped dill
1 tsp chopped garlic
Juice of 1 lemon
Salt
Ground black pepper

Any recipe with fennel goes a long way with me. It's always been one of my favourite vegetables. The anise flavour with the fresh ling cod in this recipe is a great combination. Cooking in parchment *cartoccio* concentrates the natural flavours. **Serves 6**

Preheat the oven to 400°F.

For each *cartoccio* place a sheet of parchment paper, about 14 inches long, on a flat surface. (You'll need 6 pieces of parchment paper.) In the centre of each piece place equal amounts of tomatoes, onion, fennel and garlic.

Place a ling cod fillet on top of each piece. Sprinkle 2 Tbsp of wine, plus herbs, garlic, lemon juice and salt and pepper to taste on each fillet.

Grab the corners of the parchment and bundle them to form a "purse," twisting them to seal. Place the *cartocci* on a rimmed baking sheet and bake for 10 to 12 minutes.

Serve the *cartocci* as soon as they're ready. This dish is meant to be eaten from the parchment.

HALIBUT AND OYSTER INVOLTINI

Involtini di Ippoglosso con Ostriche

Eight 2 oz pieces fresh halibut
Salt
Ground black pepper
16 Kushi oysters (or any small
  oysters), shucked
1 tsp vegetable oil
1 Tbsp butter
1 cup fresh chanterelle
  mushrooms, sliced if large
1½ cups prawn stock, or fish
  stock (page 12)

This dish was created for a winemakers' dinner when the task was to match a big, buttery Chardonnay. Have you ever had oysters like this before? **Serves 4**

Preheat the oven to 450°F. Line a rimmed baking sheet with parchment paper.

Place the halibut slices between 2 layers of waxed paper and lightly pound them to a ¼-inch thickness, 1 at a time. Remove the top layer of waxed paper and season the fish with salt and pepper.

Centre 2 oysters on each piece of halibut. Roll the halibut tightly around the oysters, leaving behind the bottom layer of waxed paper as you roll. Place the rolled halibut seam side down on the prepared baking sheet. Brush the fish very lightly with the vegetable oil and bake for 5 to 6 minutes.

Meanwhile, heat the butter in a sauté pan over medium-high heat. Add the mushrooms and season with a pinch more salt and pepper. Cook, stirring frequently, until they give off their moisture and are tender, 10 to 15 minutes. Deglaze the pan with the prawn stock and reduce for 3 or 4 minutes. Season to taste with more salt and pepper.

Serve each person 2 halibut rolls in a warm shallow bowl with hot mushroom sauce poured around them.

PISTACHIO-CRUSTED ORANGE ROUGHY
WITH FIRE-ROASTED PEPPER SAUCE

Roughy di Arancia Peperonato

ORANGE ROUGHY

Six 6 oz orange roughy steaks
2 Tbsp olive oil
1 Tbsp minced garlic
Salt
Ground black pepper
¾ cup ground pistachios

FIRE-ROASTED PEPPER SAUCE

3 shallots
3 Tbsp butter
6 roasted red bell peppers,
   peeled, seeded, chopped
3 cups chicken stock (page 10)
3 cups whipping cream
3 Tbsp honey
3 Tbsp chopped fresh basil
Salt
Ground black pepper

I first introduced this recipe in the 1980s at my restaurant Café Roma, and it's been a signature dish ever since. I've tried it with several different types of fish, and you can too, including sea bass, sablefish and halibut. The colours are beautiful—green pistachios, red pepper sauce and white fish—just like the Italian flag. **Serves 6**

Preheat the oven to 400°F. Line a baking sheet with parchment paper.

For the orange roughy, brush the fish with the olive oil, sprinkle with the garlic, season to taste with salt and pepper and roll in the ground pistachios.

Place the fish on the prepared baking sheet and bake for 10 minutes. The pistachios should be golden brown and the fish flaky.

Meanwhile, prepare the sauce. Sauté the shallots in the butter over medium-high heat for 2 minutes. Add the chopped peppers and sauté for 3 minutes. Add the chicken stock, reduce the heat to low and reduce by half. Add the cream and honey and reduce to a sauce consistency, so that the sauce coats the back of a spoon. Let the sauce cool a little then transfer it to a blender, or use a hand blender. Add the basil and purée. Season to taste with salt and pepper.

Spoon the sauce over the bottom of a warm platter and place the fish on top.

AHI TUNA WITH ANGEL HAIR PASTA

Capelli d' Angelo al Tonno

ANGEL HAIR PASTA

4 oz angel hair pasta
2 English cucumbers, peeled
1 cup bell peppers, diced
⅓ cup Champagne vinegar
½ cup extra virgin olive oil
¼ cup mirin
1 shallot, finely diced
2 Tbsp chopped fresh cilantro
Salt

TUNA

1 Tbsp Spanish paprika
2 tsp ground coriander
2 tsp dried mustard powder
1 tsp dried oregano
1 tsp chili powder
1 Tbsp brown sugar
1 tsp olive oil for searing
Six 4 oz fillets of sashimi-
   grade Ahi tuna

Angel hair is my favourite type of pasta. It's perfect when you want something fast, light and simple. This recipe is a summer menu favourite at Quattro at Whistler. It's also a new Corsi family favourite. Try it and make it one of yours too. **Serves 6**

Cook the pasta according to package directions and set it aside.

Use a mandolin or other type of slicer to cut the cucumbers into long, thin ribbons, stopping when you reach the seeds in the centre. Place the cucumber slices and bell peppers in a bowl, add the Champagne vinegar and marinate for 30 minutes.

Drain off the vinegar, reserving it for later, if necessary, to balance the seasoning. Add the olive oil, mirin, shallot, cilantro and salt to taste. Chill in the fridge, until you're ready, for several hours, but not more than a day.

For the tuna, mix together the spices and sugar and spread them on a plate.

Heat the oil over medium-high heat in a large non-stick skillet. Dip 1 side of the tuna in the spice mix and place it in the skillet. Sear the tuna for 2 to 3 minutes then flip it over. Turn off the heat and let the residual heat warm the tuna through.

Use a long-tined fork to twirl the angel hair pasta with the cucumber salad into nests in the centres of 6 plates. Thinly slice the tuna and top each nest with tuna slices.

SMOKED SABLEFISH WITH ARUGULA SALAD

Sablefish Affumicato

SABLEFISH

Six 5 oz pieces fresh (or frozen) sablefish fillets (not smoked sablefish/black cod)

2 tsp grapeseed oil

MARINADE

4 cloves garlic, roughly chopped

1 jalapeño pepper, sliced with seeds in

1 shallot, finely diced

1 bunch cilantro, roughly chopped

½ cup brown sugar, packed

½ cup orange juice

¼ cup soy sauce

1 tsp sesame oil

½ tsp liquid smoke

ARUGULA SALAD

¼ cup extra virgin olive oil

2 Tbsp Champagne vinegar

2 Tbsp grated Parmesan cheese

6–8 cups arugula

During the summer when I was writing this cookbook, my entire family visited from Italy. I have four brothers, one sister and a wonderful selection of nieces and nephews. There were over 30 of us! My nephew Stefano says this is the best piece of fish he's ever had. This sablefish isn't actually smoked, but gets its rich flavour from liquid smoke, which you should be able to find easily at specialty food stores. **Serves 6**

Score the fish skin with a small sharp knife to prevent curling during cooking.

Mix the marinade ingredients together in a non-reactive dish large enough to hold all the fish in 1 layer. Add the fish and marinate overnight, or for at least 2 hours, in the fridge.

Preheat the oven to 400°F.

Remove the sablefish from the marinade and pat it dry with paper towels.

Heat the grapeseed oil in a large, ovenproof pan over medium heat and sear the fish on all sides. Watch carefully as the residual sugar from the marinade will have a tendency to burn. Flip the fish over and transfer the pan to the oven for 6 to 8 minutes, depending on the thickness of the fish. When it's cooked, the fish will appear opaque and will flake when touched with a fork.

Meanwhile, prepare the salad. Mix together the olive oil, vinegar and cheese, whisking them with a fork.

In a large bowl toss the salad with just enough dressing to coat the arugula leaves. Place portions of salad on 6 plates and top with hot fish to wilt the greens slightly.

BAKED RAINBOW TROUT WITH BLACK TRUFFLE PASTE

Trota Tartufata

2 cups fine breadcrumbs
Zest and juice of 1 lemon
⅓ cup chopped Italian parsley
¼ cup olive oil
2 Tbsp unsalted butter, melted
Salt
Ground black pepper
6 trout fillets, pin bones
   removed
2 Tbsp vegetable oil
3 Tbsp black truffle paste

I really have to thank the Caprai winery in the village of Montefalco for this dish. I first discovered it over a wonderful lunch there and the chef graciously shared it with me. It truly highlights the best of Umbria. **Serves 6**

Mix the breadcrumbs with the lemon zest and juice, parsley, olive oil, melted butter and salt and pepper to taste.

Run a finger gently along the trout flesh and remove any stray pin bones.

Preheat the oven to 350°F.

Season the trout fillets with more salt and pepper.

Heat the vegetable oil in an ovenproof pan on medium-high heat. Place the trout in the pan, flesh side down, and pan-fry for about 2 minutes. Remove the pan from the heat and turn the trout over. Spread ½ Tbsp of truffle paste on each fillet and pat the breadcrumb mixture on the flesh side of fish.

Transfer to the oven and bake for 5 minutes.

Serve this with your favourite risotto and grilled vegetables.

GRILLED FRESH SARDINES WITH GREMOLATA
Sarde alla Gremolata

2 Tbsp chopped garlic
2 Tbsp chopped Italian parsley
1 Tbsp chopped fresh thyme
1 Tbsp chopped fresh dill
Zest and juice of 2 lemons
¼ cup extra virgin olive oil
   + extra for brushing on
   sardines
12 whole fresh sardines,
   cleaned and butterflied with
   the backbone removed (your
   fishmonger will perform this
   task, if asked)
Salt
Ground black pepper

Can't you just feel the salty sea spray on your face? Sardines have a way of transporting me back to the coast of Italy. **Serves 6**

In a stainless steel bowl, make gremolata by mixing the garlic, herbs, lemon zest and juice with the ¼ cup of olive oil to form a loose paste.

Preheat the grill to medium-high.

Season the flesh side of the sardines with salt and pepper and brush them lightly with olive oil to prevent them from sticking on the grill.

Place the sardines flesh side down on the grill and cook them for 2 minutes. Flip them over, brush them with the gremolata and cook for another 3 to 4 minutes. Transfer them from the grill to serving plates. You can spread more gremolata on the cooked fish if you like.

Serve warm.

CLASS | *Vongole*

There are so many wonderful ways to enjoy clams, but the next two recipes are a couple of my favourites.

CLAMS WITH WHITE WINE
Vongole all' Origano

3 lb clams, rinsed thoroughly
   under cold, running water for
   about 5 minutes to flush out
   any sand
2 Tbsp extra virgin olive oil
½ yellow onion, diced
2 Tbsp finely chopped garlic
1 Tbsp peperoncino
1 cup dry white wine
1 cup tomato sauce (page 15)
3 Tbsp chopped Italian parsley

Serves 6

Inspect the rinsed clams, discarding any that are open and won't close when tapped.

Heat the olive oil in a large skillet on medium-high heat. Sauté the onion, garlic and peperoncino for 3 minutes. Add the clams and deglaze the pan with the white wine. Add the tomato sauce, bring to a boil, cover the pan, reduce the heat and simmer until the clams are open, 4 to 5 minutes.

Discard any clams that did not open when cooked.

Ladle the clams and their sauce into a large, warm bowl and sprinkle them with Italian parsley.

CLANS WITH VERMOUTH

Vongole al Vermouth

3 lb clams, rinsed thoroughly
   under cold, running water for
   about 5 minutes to flush out
   any sand
2 Tbsp extra virgin olive oil
1 cup chopped green olives
2 Tbsp chopped garlic
1 Tbsp peperoncino
1 cup vermouth
1 cup fish stock (page 12) or
   clam nectar
2 Tbsp chopped fresh oregano

Serves 6

Inspect the rinsed clams, discarding any that are open and won't close when tapped.

Heat the oil in a large skillet over medium-high heat. Sauté the olives, garlic and peperoncino for 2 minutes. Add the clams and deglaze the pan with the vermouth. Reduce for 2 minutes. Add the fish stock, cover the pan, reduce the heat and simmer until the clams are open, 4 to 5 minutes.

Discard any clams that did not open when cooked.

Finish with fresh oregano and serve in warm bowls with crusty Italian bread.

MUSSELS | *Cozze*

The best mussels I ever tasted were from Saltspring Island. They were plump little pillows from the sea. Try the next two recipes on their own or atop a seafood risotto.

MUSSELS IN RED SAUCE

Cozze al Pomodoro

3 lb fresh mussels, well washed and debearded
2 Tbsp extra virgin olive oil
3 anchovy fillets, diced
½ onion, diced
2 Tbsp chopped garlic
1 Tbsp peperoncino
1 cup dry white wine
2 cups tomato sauce (page 15)
Salt
Ground black pepper
3 Tbsp chiffonade of fresh basil

Serves 6

Inspect the mussels, discarding any with broken shells or open ones that do not close when tapped.

Heat the olive oil in a large skillet over medium-high heat and sauté the anchovies, onion, garlic and peperoncino for 2 minutes. Add the mussels and deglaze the pan with the white wine. Add the tomato sauce, bring to a boil, reduce the heat and cover the pan. Cook until the mussels open, 5 to 6 minutes.

Remove the pan from the heat and discard any mussels that don't open. Season the sauce to taste with salt and pepper.

Transfer the mussels to a large, warm bowl and sprinkle with the fresh basil chiffonade.

MUSSELS WITH CREAM SAUCE

Cozze Alla Crema

3 lb fresh mussels, well
    washed and debearded
1 cup washed, julienned leeks,
    white and light green parts
    only
2 Tbsp chopped garlic
1 Tbsp peperoncino
1 Tbsp butter
1 cup dry white wine
1 cup whipping cream
Juice of 1 lemon
2 Tbsp chopped fresh dill

Serves 6

Inspect the mussels, discarding any with broken shells or open ones that do not close when tapped.

In a large skillet over medium-high heat, sauté the leeks, garlic and peperoncino in the butter for 2 minutes, stirring. Add the mussels and deglaze the pan with the white wine. Cook, covered, until the mussels open, 5 to 6 minutes. Transfer the mussels with a slotted spoon to a large bowl. Discard any that do not open after cooking.

Add the cream to the skillet and reduce until the sauce thickens. Add the fresh lemon juice and chopped dill then return the mussels to the pan and heat them in the sauce.

Serve hot.

SPOT PRAWNS IN VERMOUTH SAUCE
Gamberetti al Vermouth

3 whole cloves of garlic
  (crushed)
3 Tbsp salted butter
3 lb spot prawns (seasonal),
  peeled and deveined
⅔ cup white vermouth
3 Tbsp chopped Italian parsley
1 Tbsp chili flakes
Juice of 1 lemon
3 Tbsp cold salted butter cut
  in ½-inch cubes
Salt
Ground black pepper

It doesn't get any better than BC spot prawns served with Mediterranean flair. **Serves 6**

Over medium heat sauté the garlic in the salted butter for 1 minute. Remove the garlic and increase the heat to high.

Add the prawns and sauté them for 2 minutes. Add the vermouth and cook for 2 more minutes. Sprinkle with the parsley, chili flakes and lemon juice.

Transfer the prawns to a platter. Into the remaining liquid in the pan, whisk the cold butter cubes to form a sauce (*monté au beurre*). Season to taste with salt and pepper. Pour the sauce over the prawns.

POACHED OCTOPUS WITH CANNELLINI BEANS

Polpo con Fagioli

4 lb baby octopus

4 bay leaves

2 whole cloves of garlic

1 Tbsp whole black
 peppercorns

1 tsp salt

1 Tbsp extra virgin olive oil

4 bell peppers, 2 yellow and
 2 red, cut in julienne strips

1 Tbsp chopped garlic

Two 12 oz cans cannellini
 beans, rinsed and drained

1 sprig rosemary

1 sprig sage

Salt

Ground black pepper

¼ cup balsamic vinegar or a
 squeeze of fresh lemon juice
 for each plate

¼ cup extra virgin olive oil

Recipes that are best served at room temperature, like this one, are perfect for entertaining. It's such a shame that octopus is usually overlooked, because it's so delicious. Don't over-cook it and you'll enjoy its delectable flavour and texture to the max. **Serves 6**

Place the octopus in a large pot, cover it with cold water and add the bay leaves, garlic, peppercorns and salt. Bring to a boil, reduce the heat, cover and simmer gently until the octopus is tender, about 15 minutes. The cooking time for octopus can vary widely. Check to see if it's tender starting at 15 minutes and every few minutes after that. Remove the pot from the heat and let the octopus cool in its poaching liquid. Once cool, remove from the poaching liquid and set aside.

Heat the olive oil in a sauté pan over medium heat and cook the peppers with the chopped garlic for 2 to 3 minutes. Add the beans, rosemary and sage. Season to taste with salt and pepper if necessary. If the beans are dry, add some of the octopus poaching liquid to moisten them. Remove the beans from the heat and let them cool slightly. Add the cooked octopus and mix everything together.

Drizzle each serving with balsamic vinegar or fresh lemon juice, and extra virgin olive oil. This dish is served warm or at room temperature, not hot.

POULTRY, GAME
AND MEAT

*Pollame, Selvaggina
e Carne*

BRICK-FLATTENED CORNISH GAME HEN

Galletto al Mattone

4 game hens (ask your butcher
  to debone them)
1 tsp cayenne pepper
Salt
Ground black pepper
¼ cup chopped fresh rosemary
½ cup fresh basil, torn into
  pieces
⅓ cup chopped fresh oregano
2 Tbsp chopped fresh sage
2 Tbsp chopped fresh thyme
2 cups extra virgin olive oil
2 Tbsp chopped garlic
1 tsp chili flakes

This was one of my nonna's most popular dishes. She used to make bread once a week in her wood-burning oven, and while the oven was fired up she would prepare this with free-range chickens that we got to select ourselves. "Which one do you like?" she would ask us. This is a modern application of one of my favourite dishes as a kid. The flavours are so authentic I swear I'm back in Rome when I eat this. **Serves 4, or up to 8 if the hens are large**

Sprinkle the game hens with the cayenne pepper and salt and pepper to taste. Combine the herbs and olive oil in a container large enough to hold them and the hens. Marinate the hens, covered, in the fridge for 6 to 8 hours, or up to overnight.

Remove the hens from the marinade. Pat them dry with paper towels and rub them with the garlic and chili flakes.

Prepare four 6 lb clay bricks, about 8½ × 4 × 2½ inches each, by cleaning them well and wrapping them individually in 2 layers of tinfoil.

Heat the bricks for 30 minutes on a medium-heat grill.

Place the hens on the grill, skin side down. Cover them with a flat pan and place the hot bricks on top. Grill over medium heat for 15 to 20 minutes, turning the birds over halfway through the cooking time. Allow the hens to rest on a cutting board for 5 minutes, with the breasts down and legs raised so that the juices run back into the breast meat. Large birds can be cut down the centre to make 2 servings each.

Serve with a squeeze of fresh lemon juice, grilled vegetables and roast potatoes.

If boneless hens are not available, cut out the backbone with kitchen shears and flatten the birds with the heel of your hand. This dish is tastiest if you can marinate the birds overnight, and it's great when cooked on a panini grill.

ROAST QUAIL WITH TUSCAN CANNELLINI BEAN SALAD

Quaglie con Fagioli

BEAN SALAD

2 cups dry cannellini beans, or two 14 oz cans rinsed and drained
8 cups water or vegetable stock (page 14)
2 Tbsp butter
1 onion, diced
5 cloves garlic, chopped
½ cup chopped fresh basil
¼ cup grated Parmesan cheese
3½ oz sliced pancetta, cooked crisp, drained on paper towels
Salt
Ground black pepper

QUAIL

1 tsp salt
½ cup chopped fresh basil
¼ cup chopped fresh rosemary
Cracked black pepper
½ tsp cayenne pepper
2 tsp extra virgin olive oil
6 boneless quail
Juice of 2 lemons

Talk about simple family food memories. This is a version of a recipe my brother Mario and my mother used to make. Mario would go hunting and catch the bird, we would harvest beans from our garden and my mother would make this dish. Start cooking this on the morning of or day before serving. **Serves 6**

Cover the beans in cold water and soak them for at least 6 hours.

Drain the soaked beans, cover them with the fresh water or vegetable stock and cook partially covered and without salt, until al dente, about 40 minutes to 1 hour. Drain and reserve any cooking liquid.

Melt the butter in a saucepan on medium-low heat and cook the onion until it's translucent and soft but not browned. Add the garlic and cook for 2 to 3 minutes. Stir in the drained beans and ¼ cup of the reserved bean liquid, if using dried beans, and cook the beans on low heat until just soft but not falling apart.

Stir in the basil, Parmesan and crumbled crisp pancetta and season to taste with salt and pepper just before serving.

Preheat the oven to 350°F.

For the quail, mix together the salt, herbs, pepper to taste and cayenne pepper and rub them evenly over the quail.

Heat the oil in an ovenproof skillet and sear the quail until they're golden brown on both sides. Roast for 8 minutes. Remove and let rest on a cutting board for 2 minutes.

Squeeze the lemon juice over the quail and serve with the hot bean salad.

POACHED AND STUFFED CHICKEN

Pollo Ripieno

½ rustic Italian loaf of bread,
   crusts removed, cut in
   2-inch cubes
2 cups whole milk
3 lb whole chicken with heart
   and liver
3 Italian sausages, skins
   removed, chopped
1 egg
3 Tbsp salted butter, melted
2 Tbsp chopped Italian parsley
1 Tbsp chopped garlic
¼ cup Marsala
Salt
Ground black pepper
16 cups chicken stock
   (page 10)

This is a very old-fashioned way of cooking; my mother used to make this for us. She'd stuff and poach the chicken for dinner and then make a wonderful soup the next day. If you're looking for an excellent roast chicken recipe, prepare and stuff the chicken then brush it with butter or olive oil and roast it in the oven. **Serves 6**

Soak the bread in the milk for 30 minutes. Squeeze and discard the excess milk from the bread and place the bread in a large bowl.

Add the chicken heart and liver, sausages, egg, butter, parsley, garlic and Marsala. Season salt and pepper if necessary.

Stuff the chicken and close it up with skewers and kitchen string. Place it in a large pot and cover with the chicken stock. Bring to a boil, cover and reduce the heat to keep the stock at a gentle simmer. The chicken will take about 1 hour to cook. The breast meat should reach 160°F and the thigh meat should reach 165°F.

Any extra stuffing can be baked in a small ramekin until the juices run clear yellow. Strain and save the flavourful chicken poaching liquid for use in soup recipes.

CHICKEN WITH LIVER AND TOMATO

Petto di Pollo al Fegato

Six 8 oz chicken breasts,
  boneless, skinless
¼ cup extra virgin olive oil,
  divided
1 Tbsp chopped garlic
1 Tbsp chopped fresh
  rosemary
1 Tbsp chopped fresh sage
1 lb chicken liver, roughly
  chopped
2 cups white wine, preferably
  riesling
4 Roma tomatoes, peeled,
  seeded, cut in ½-inch dice
  (1 cup tomato concasse)
2 bay leaves
Salt
Ground black pepper
2 Tbsp finely chopped Italian
  parsley

This is a tasty dish, even for those who normally don't enjoy liver. **Serves 8 (or more)**

Marinate the chicken in 2 Tbsp of the olive oil, the garlic, rosemary and sage for 2 hours, in the fridge.

Preheat the oven to 375°F.

Remove the chicken from the marinade. Heat the remaining oil in an ovenproof skillet on medium-high heat and sear the chicken breasts, about 3 to 4 minutes per side. Add the chopped chicken liver, riesling, tomato concasse and bay leaves. Bring to a boil on the stovetop over medium-high heat.

Cover and transfer to the oven for 20 to 30 minutes until the chicken's cooked through. Remove from the oven and discard the bay leaves. Season to taste with salt and pepper.

Transfer the chicken to a large serving platter, and garnish with the parsley before serving.

DRUNKEN CHICKEN
Pollo Ubriaco

6 chicken thighs, bone in (skin removed if you prefer)
6 chicken breasts, bone in
Salt
Ground black pepper
2 Tbsp extra virgin olive oil
10 slices prosciutto, cut in julienne strips
2 red bell peppers, cut in julienne strips
1 large onion, cut in julienne strips
2 Tbsp chopped garlic
4 Roma tomatoes, peeled, seeded, cut in ½-inch dice (1 cup tomato concasse)
1 cup dry white wine
½ cup brandy
½ cup port
¼ cup Dijon mustard
2 cups veal stock (page 11)
2 Tbsp chopped Italian parsley

Make this recipe along with a big pot of minestrone when you're stuck inside during a snowstorm or on any wintry day. This recipe is especially generous so it's a good one if you're feeding a hungry crowd. **Serves 6–8**

Preheat the oven to 375°F.

Season the chicken pieces with salt and pepper. Heat the olive oil in a roasting pan on the stovetop and brown the chicken on all sides.

Remove the chicken from the pan and set it aside. Chicken with its skin on will render extra fat. Discard all but 1 Tbsp of the fat from the pan before sautéing the vegetables.

Add the prosciutto, peppers, onion and garlic to the pan and sauté them, stirring, for 3 minutes. Stir in the tomato concasse, white wine, brandy and port, and whisk in the Dijon mustard. Reduce for 3 minutes at medium-high heat to cook away some of the alcohol to concentrate the flavours. Add the veal stock, Italian parsley and browned chicken, bring to a boil, cover and roast in the oven for 30 minutes. Remove the cover and roast for a further 15 minutes before serving.

BEER CHICKEN
Pollo alla Birra

2 Tbsp extra virgin olive oil
2 shallots, cut in ½-inch dice
2 stalks celery, cut in ½-inch dice
1 carrot, cut in ½-inch dice
Six 6 oz pieces chicken breast, bone in, skin on
1 tsp cumin seeds
Salt
Ground black pepper
Two 12 oz cans lager beer, divided
4 Yukon Gold potatoes, cut in 1-inch dice, about 3 cups
1 clove garlic, peeled
2 Tbsp extra virgin olive oil
1 sprig rosemary

This recipe is a great one to serve when you're having friends over to watch a sports game. It's a natural with beer. Be sure to serve plenty of fresh bread alongside so that you can soak up the delicious juices. In Italian we say *scarpetta*, which means small shoe. I love to see my little granddaughter using her bread *scarpetta* to get to the very last drop of her favourite foods. **Serves 6–8**

Preheat the oven to 375°F.

Heat the oil in a large skillet with a lid and sauté the shallots, celery and carrot for 3 minutes. Push the vegetables to the side of the pan and add the chicken, skin side down. Brown both sides and add the cumin seeds, salt and pepper to taste and 1 can of the beer. Bring the liquid to a boil, reduce the heat to low, cover and cook until the chicken is tender and juices run clear yellow. Monitor the liquid level, adding more beer as necessary. Remove the chicken when it's cooked, 25 to 30 minutes. Increase the heat to high and reduce the sauce until it's syrupy, about 10 minutes.

Meanwhile, place the potatoes, garlic, oil and rosemary in a roasting pan or a baking sheet lined with tinfoil. Roast for 30 to 40 minutes until the potatoes are crispy on the outside and tender in the middle. Reduce the heat if the potatoes are too brown. Discard the rosemary stem.

To serve, transfer the potatoes from the oven to a warm platter and arrange the chicken on top. Pour the sauce overtop the chicken pieces.

TURKEY BURGERS FRANCESCO
Hamburger alla Francesco

1 lb medium lean ground
turkey

2 medium carrots, peeled,
chopped in ⅛-inch dice

½ medium red bell pepper,
chopped in ⅛-inch dice

½ medium yellow bell pepper,
chopped in ⅛-inch dice

½ medium white onion,
chopped in ⅛-inch dice

½ medium red onion, chopped
in ⅛-inch dice

1 egg

1½ cups fresh Italian
breadcrumbs, divided

½ cup shredded cheddar
cheese

½ cup shredded mozzarella
cheese

1 tsp salt

Ground black pepper

My friend David, whom I call Francesco, doesn't know how to cook. This is the only dish that he makes, and he serves it every chance he gets. Good thing it's so delicious. We always enjoy these a day after as a snack on the golf course. Great with Pinot Grigio. **Serves 6**

In a large stainless steel mixing bowl, place the ground turkey and add the chopped carrots, peppers and onions. Mix together with a potato masher. Add the egg and mix until the egg is absorbed. Add ½ cup of the breadcrumbs and mix them in well. Add both cheeses and mix again. Add the remaining 1 cup breadcrumbs, season with salt and pepper and combine thoroughly.

Preheat the barbecue to high.

Divide the mixture in 12 and form into 2½-inch round balls. Use your hands to toss the mixture back and forth and firm it up. Flatten the balls into a burger shape.

Reduce the barbecue to low then spray the grill with non-stick spray or brush it with olive oil.

Place the burgers on the grill and cook each side for 5 minutes twice, for a total cooking time of 20 minutes.

TURKEY BREAST WITH FRESH MOZZARELLA

Tacchino Caprese

1 bay leaf

2 sprigs thyme

2 sprigs sage

6 sprigs Italian parsley

1 Tbsp whole black
peppercorns

1 tsp salt

1 turkey breast, boneless,
skinless, about 3 lb

1 Tbsp salted butter for
greasing

4 ripe Roma tomatoes, peeled,
seeded, cut in ½-inch dice
(1 cup tomato concasse)

8 balls of bocconcini, sliced
½-inch thick

2 Tbsp chiffonade of fresh
basil

Turkey's not just for Christmas or Thanksgiving, and tomatoes and mozzarella go way beyond *caprese* salad. **Serves 6**

Wrap the herbs and peppercorns together in cheesecloth and place it in 20 cups of cold water with the salt and turkey breast. Bring to a boil then reduce the heat. Simmer gently for 20 to 25 minutes, or until the turkey breast is cooked to an internal temperature of 170°F. Remove the turkey from the cooking liquid and let it cool.

Preheat the oven to 400°F.

Slice the turkey breast ¼ inch thick and lay the slices in a lightly buttered casserole dish big enough to hold all the ingredients without crowding. Sprinkle the tomato concasse overtop and layer with the bocconcini slices.

Bake for 10 to 12 minutes, or until the bocconcini is melted. Remove from the oven and sprinkle with the chiffonade of fresh basil before serving.

ROASTED DUCK BREAST WITH MAPLE AND GRILLED APPLE *SUCCO*

Anitra Melata

6 Brome Lake duck breasts, about 7 oz each
½ cup maple syrup
¼ cup brandy
1 Granny Smith apple, cored and sliced
1 cup chicken stock (page 10)
Salt
Cracked black pepper
¼ cup sliced toasted almonds

I came up with this recipe just to satisfy the need for duck on the menu. Duck isn't common in Rome, so this dish isn't really very Italian. With the maple syrup it's a tribute to Canada, my other home. The leftovers make a wonderful salad for a great lunch.

Duck isn't easy to cook, so most people don't at home. It has to be done perfectly otherwise it gets dry. Brome Lake ducks, a cross between Long Island and Peking ducks, from Montreal, are smaller than their Muscovy cousins so cook more quickly. **Serves 6**

Preheat the oven to 350°F.

Score the duck skin in a grid pattern. Place the duck, skin side down, in a dry ovenproof pan over medium heat. Render the fat until the skin is crispy and golden. Turn the breasts over and transfer them to the oven to roast for 10 minutes, or until medium rare. Remove the pan from the oven and transfer the duck from the pan. Let the duck rest, loosely covered in tinfoil to keep warm.

Place the hot pan on medium heat and deglaze it with the maple syrup and brandy. Add the apple slices and chicken stock, reducing the sauce and cooking the apples until they're tender but still holding their shape, 8 to 10 minutes. When the sauce is syrupy, season it to taste with salt and pepper.

Slice the duck breast and fan it out on plates or 1 large platter. Spoon sauce and apples overtop and sprinkle with the almonds.

Serve with polenta, or mashed or roasted potatoes.

FRANGELICO DUCK BREAST

Anitra al Frangelico

3 Muscovy duck breasts,
   about 1 lb each
Salt
Ground black pepper
2 Tbsp Frangelico
1 cup chicken stock (page 10)
2 Tbsp cold butter
¼ cup toasted pine nuts
3 or 4 grilled orange slices

This is duck with an Italian twist. I love the flavour of duck and nuts together. Duck à l'orange is, of course, the most popular duck dish of all time, and it's the inspiration behind this recipe. Blood oranges work wonderfully in this dish when they're in season. **Serves 6–8**

Score the duck skin in a grid pattern. Season the meat with salt and pepper and place skin side down in a dry skillet over medium heat. Slowly render the fat until the skin is golden and crisp. Pour off any excess fat (and save it for roasting potatoes).

Flip the duck breast over, add the Frangelico and flambé (see sidebar page 160). Add the chicken stock and cook the duck at a light simmer until medium rare, 7 to 10 minutes. Test the duck with the point of a knife. The juices should run pink and the duck should offer some resistance when it's pressed with a finger.

Remove the duck from the pan and allow it to rest. Reduce the sauce until it's syrupy, about 5 minutes. Add the cold butter and whisk until it's smooth. Season to taste with more salt and pepper.

Fan thin slices of duck on each plate or 1 large platter, or present the duck breasts whole, and top them with the pine nuts, grilled orange slices and the sauce.

PHEASANT WITH CHANTERELLE CREAM
Fagiano con Finferli

1 medium spaghetti squash,
    split in half lengthwise,
    seeds removed
Six 5 oz pheasant breasts (or
    free-range chicken breasts
    or quail)
Salt
Ground black pepper
2 Tbsp olive oil, divided
12–15 fresh chanterelle
    mushrooms
1 cup chicken stock (page 10)
¼ cup brandy
1 cup whipping cream
5 cloves garlic, minced,
    divided
1 small white truffle (or 1 tsp
    white truffle oil)
1 bunch rapini, blanched,
    drained, roughly chopped

This is a true Tuscan combination. If you can't find pheasant, try using quail or free-range chicken breast. **Serves 6**

Preheat the oven to 350°F.

Place the squash cut side down in a roasting pan containing enough water to cover the bottom of the pan. Cover with tinfoil and roast until tender, 35 to 40 minutes. Remove the squash from the pan and cool. Once it's cooled, use a fork to pull the flesh away in long, spaghetti-like strands. Set the strands aside.

Increase the oven to 400°F.

Season the pheasant with salt and pepper.

Heat 1 Tbsp of the olive oil in a roasting pan on the stovetop. Place the pheasant, skin side down, in the hot oil and sear it until it's golden. Flip it over, transfer it to the oven and roast it for 7 to 10 minutes. The pheasant should be just cooked through; any longer will overcook the meat, leaving it dry. Set aside to rest.

Return the roasting pan to the stovetop over medium-high heat. Sauté the chanterelles briefly in the hot pan before deglazing it with the chicken stock. Add the brandy and flambé (see sidebar page 160). Add the cream and reduce until the sauce coats the back of a spoon.

Heat the squash in a saucepan in 1 tsp of the olive oil and half the minced garlic. Season with more salt and pepper, and a few slices of the truffle or a drizzle of truffle oil.

Sauté the rapini in the remaining 2 tsp olive oil and the remaining garlic until it's heated through. Season to taste with more salt and pepper.

Place some squash in the centre of each plate and spoon rapini overtop. Stack sliced pheasant breast on top of the rapini and drizzle with sauce.

PORK CHOPS WITH OLIVES

Costolette di Maiale con Olive

6 pork chops
Salt
Ground black pepper
All-purpose white flour for
 dusting
2 Tbsp olive oil
1 bay leaf
¾ cup dry white wine
½ cup green Bella di Cerignola
 olives, chopped
2 Tbsp black olive paste
1 tsp chili flakes

Try to find locally raised pork at your favourite grocery store or butcher. It makes quite a big difference. This recipe is nice with simple roast potatoes and a salad. **Serves 6**

Season the chops with salt and pepper then dust them with flour, shaking off any excess. In a sauté pan, heat the olive oil with the bay leaf over medium-high heat for 1 minute. Add the pork chops and brown them, 4 to 5 minutes per side. If the bay leaf starts to break or burn, simply remove it. It will have flavoured the oil by this time.

Deglaze the pan with the white wine then add the olives, olive paste and chili flakes. Simmer lightly until the pork is cooked. Pork is safe to eat while slightly pink and still juicy at 140–150°F. Taste the sauce and season to taste with more salt and pepper.

Transfer the pork to a warm platter and pour the olive sauce overtop.

ROAST PORK TENDERLOIN WITH GRAPPA AND SUN-DRIED CHERRIES

Filetto di Maiale alla Grappa

3 cloves garlic, minced

2 Tbsp chopped fresh sage

¾ cup + 1 Tbsp olive oil

Salt

Cayenne pepper

2 whole pork tenderloins, cleaned (about 1 lb each)

1 Tbsp olive oil

¼ cup grappa

2 Tbsp chopped sun-dried cherries

½ cup chicken stock (page 10)

¼ cup Amarena cherry syrup (see recipe intro page 52)

¼ cup red wine vinegar

1 Tbsp butter

This recipe takes me full circle as a restaurateur. It's a flashback to my flambé days at the Park Royal Hotel as well as a testament to the wonderful grappa collection we have at Quattro today. If you haven't tried grappa before, brace yourself. It's an experience. **Serves 6**

Mix together the garlic, sage and ¾ cup olive oil in a non-reactive container large enough to hold the mixture and the pork. Mix in salt and cayenne pepper to taste. Marinate the pork for 1 hour at room temperature.

Remove the pork from the marinade and pat it dry with paper towels.

Preheat the oven to 400°F.

Heat the 1 Tbsp olive oil in an ovenproof pan. Sear the pork on all sides then transfer it to the oven for 6 to 8 minutes. The pork will be juiciest if its internal temperature does not exceed 145°F. Remove the pork and set aside to rest on a cutting board.

Return the pan to the stove, and add the grappa and sun-dried cherries and flambé (see sidebar). When the flames die down, add the chicken stock, cherry syrup and red wine vinegar and reduce by half. Whisk in the butter to finish the sauce.

Slice the pork tenderloin and serve it with the cherry sauce.

To flambé a dish, simply light a match and hold it near the surface of the dish or sauce to ignite immediately. When the flames die down you can add any remaining ingredients.

BUFFALO LOIN IN PALE ALE

Bufalo alla Birra

1½ lb buffalo loin
Two 12 oz bottles pale ale
5 dried juniper berries
2 bay leaves
Salt
Ground black pepper
All-purpose white flour for
  dusting
2 Tbsp salted butter
2 cups vegetable stock
  (page 14)
1 cup halved seedless green
  grapes

My uncle who lived in Maenza, just outside of Rome, raised buffalo while I was growing up. Originally this recipe was made with red wine, which makes for a very earthy and satisfying dish. Substitute the wine with pale ale and you have much lighter, more modern fare. **Serves 6**

In a non-reactive container marinate the buffalo loin for 2 hours in the pale ale, juniper berries and bay leaves.

Remove the buffalo, reserving the marinade, and season with salt and pepper and dust with the flour.

In a sauté pan over medium-high heat, melt the butter and brown the buffalo, 2 to 3 minutes on each side. Add the reserved marinade and reduce the volume by half.

Remove the buffalo if it's cooked to medium-rare (internal temperature of 130–135°F) at this point. If not, leave the buffalo in the sauce and turn it frequently until it finishes cooking. Allow it to rest on a carving board while the sauce reduces further to a syrupy consistency. Increase the heat to high and add the vegetable stock. Reduce until the sauce is lightly syrupy.

Add the grapes and season to taste with more salt and pepper. Heat the grapes through in the sauce, about 2 minutes.

Slice the buffalo loin, arrange on a warm platter and ladle grape sauce overtop.

ROASTED LAMB WITH OLIVES

Agnello Oliveto

OLIVE *SUCCO*

2 tsp olive oil

¾ cup black Taggiasche olives,
  pitted and cut in half (or
  mild black olives)

2 cups Cabernet Sauvignon

1½ cups veal stock (page 11)

Salt

Ground black pepper

1 tsp honey, if necessary to
  balance taste

2 Tbsp butter

1 Tbsp chopped fresh thyme

LAMB

6 pieces 6–7 oz lamb loins

1 Tbsp olive oil, divided

¼ cup grainy Dijon mustard

3 Tbsp smooth Dijon mustard

1 Tbsp chopped garlic

1 Tbsp chopped rosemary

Pinch cayenne pepper

Salt

Ground black pepper

This is a wonderful dish to serve your family at Easter. Or consider it for a Christmas dinner Corsi-style, because lamb is a classic choice for Christmas dinner in central Italy where I'm from. Serve this with roast potatoes and roasted bell peppers. If you can't find Taggiasche olives, kalamata or other black olives would work. **Serves 6–8**

For the *succo*, in a 6-cup saucepan heat the olive oil over medium heat then lightly sauté the olives for 2 to 3 minutes. Add the red wine and reduce until it's almost dry. Stir in the veal stock and reduce until the mixture is slightly syrupy. This could take 20 minutes but you need to watch it carefully while it reduces.

Season to taste with salt, pepper and, if necessary, honey. Whisk in the butter and add the fresh thyme.

Bring the lamb to room temperature and rub it all over with 1 tsp of the olive oil. Preheat the oven to 400°F.

Mix together the mustards, garlic, rosemary and cayenne pepper. Set aside.

Season the lamb with salt and pepper. Heat a 12-inch ovenproof sauté pan (or 2 smaller pans) over medium-high heat. Add the remaining olive oil to the hot pan and sear the lamb loins until they're well browned. Spread mustard mixture on the top side only of each loin.

Roast in the oven for 5 or 6 minutes until the internal temperature is 135°F for medium rare. Transfer the lamb to a cutting board and allow it to rest, uncovered, for at least 5 minutes before carving.

Slice the lamb and arrange the slices on warm plates with olive *succo* ladled overtop, but with most of the lamb showing through.

RACK OF LAMB WITH MARSALA AND DRIED FIGS

Costolette d'Agnello al Marsala

Two 8-rib Canadian lamb racks
  (Frenched)
½ cup dried Mediterranean
  figs, about 6
¼ cup Marsala or port
Salt
Ground black pepper
1 Tbsp vegetable oil
1 cup veal demi-glace
  (page 11)
1 Tbsp grainy Dijon mustard
1 Tbsp very finely chopped
  fresh rosemary

I love figs, but it can be difficult to find really good dried ones here. Pick your figs carefully and they'll reward you sweetly and softly. This combination with lamb is common in the countryside surrounding Rome, where I grew up seeing shepherds tending their flocks. The Marsala gives the dish its spark. It's tart and sweet and balances the pungent lamb flavour. Be sure to buy your lamb from a source close to home. We have excellent lamb in BC.

Serves 6

Remove the lamb from the fridge 1 hour before cooking. Cut the figs into quarters and soak them in the Marsala for about 1 hour.

Preheat the oven to 350°F.

Season the lamb with salt and pepper. Heat the oil in an ovenproof sauté pan on medium-high heat. When the oil is barely smoking, sear the lamb on all sides to a rich brown then transfer it to the oven for 10 to 12 minutes, until medium rare (the internal temperature of the thickest part should be 135–140°F). Rest the lamb, uncovered, on a carving board for 5 minutes before cutting it.

Place the sauté pan on the stovetop over medium heat, add the figs and Marsala and flambé (see sidebar page 160). When the flames die down, add the demi-glace, mustard and rosemary. Stir the brown bits off the bottom of the pan and increase the heat to reduce for 5 minutes. When the sauce thickens slightly, season to taste with more salt and pepper.

Cut the lamb into chops, arrange on warm plates or a large, warm platter and drizzle with the sauce.

Serve this with mashed potatoes and vegetables of your choice.

Promise me you'll eat the lamb properly—with your fingers. Please don't use a fork and knife. In Italy we say *scottadito*, which means "burned fingertips."

LAMB CHOPS WITH EGGPLANT CAPONATA
Braciolette Simonetta

LAMB CHOPS

18 small lamb chops
1 Tbsp olive oil
1 Tbsp chopped fresh
   rosemary
1 Tbsp peperoncino
1 Tbsp finely chopped garlic
Salt
Ground black pepper

EGGPLANT CAPONATA

1 large or 2 small eggplant
Kosher salt for sprinkling
¼ cup olive oil
¾ cup sultana raisins
¼ cup finely diced onion
1 Tbsp granulated sugar
¼ cup white wine vinegar
3 Tbsp chopped fresh oregano
Salt
Ground black pepper

This recipe was inspired by a good friend's mother back in Sicily. Sweet-and-sour combinations like this are very common in Southern Italy. I hope this recipe is as good as the original. Ciao, Mamma Simonetta! **Serves 6–8**

Rub the lamb chops with the olive oil, rosemary, peperoncino and garlic. Leave them to marinate at room temperature for about 1 hour before cooking.

Line a baking tray with paper towel.

For the caponata, peel and cut the eggplant into 1-inch pieces and lay them on the prepared baking tray. Sprinkle the pieces with kosher salt and let them sit for 15 to 20 minutes to release the moisture. Wipe the eggplant pieces dry.

In a 10-inch sauté pan, heat the olive oil to just below smoking point. Add the eggplant and sauté, stirring, over medium-high heat for 5 or 6 minutes. Add the raisins, onion and sugar and cook for 2 minutes. Increase the heat to high and add the white wine vinegar. Cook until the eggplant is tender, stirring frequently. Add the oregano and salt and pepper to taste. The caponata can be served hot or at room temperature.

For the lamb, preheat the grill to medium high. (Or use a ridged grill pan on the stovetop or broiler.)

Season the lamb chops with salt and pepper and grill to the desired doneness. Depending on the thickness of the lamb, 4 to 5 minutes per side should give you medium rare.

Place the grilled lamb chops on a warm platter accompanied by the caponata in a serving bowl.

VEAL SCALOPPINE WITH VODKA

Scaloppine Russe

2 Tbsp butter
2 shallots, finely diced
12 pieces Provimi veal
   scaloppine, about 3 oz each
⅓ cup vodka
2 cups veal stock (page 11)
¼ cup Dijon mustard
4 Roma tomatoes, peeled,
   seeded, cut in ½-inch dice
   (1 cup tomato concasse)
1 cup whipping cream
Salt
Ground black pepper

This recipe was a hit at Corsi Trattoria. In the early '80s scaloppine was very popular, and this one was always a winner. **Serves 6**

Over medium-high heat in a large skillet, melt the butter and sauté the shallots for 2 minutes. Push them to the side of the pan and sear the scaloppine for about 2 minutes on each side.

Transfer the veal to a plate and deglaze the pan with the vodka. Add the veal stock and reduce by half. Whisk in the Dijon mustard. Stir in the tomato concasse and cream and reduce until the sauce coats the back of a spoon. Taste and season with salt and pepper if necessary.

Return the scaloppine to the pan, spooning sauce overtop and cooking for a few minutes until the scaloppine are heated through.

VEAL LOINS WITH LEMON ZEST

Medaglioni di Vitello al Limone

VEAL

Six 5 oz veal strip loins
  (Provimi if available)
Salt
Ground black pepper
1 Tbsp extra virgin olive oil

SAUCE

2 shallots, finely diced
2 lemons, the zest from 1 and
  the juice from both lemons,
  divided
2 cups dry Chardonnay
¼ cup salted butter, cold, cut
  in small cubes
2 Tbsp finely chopped Italian
  parsley

Italians typically eat more veal than beef, and my favourite part is the strip loin. This dish is ideal served with rapini, broccoli or even sautéed spinach. Serves 6

Preheat the oven to 375°F.

Season the veal with salt and pepper. Heat the olive oil in an ovenproof pan on medium-high heat and sear the veal for 3 to 4 minutes on each side until browned. Transfer the veal to the oven for about 10 minutes, or until its internal temperature reaches 135–140°F. Remove the pan from the oven and let the meat rest on a carving board while you make the sauce.

For the sauce, sauté the shallots in the roasting pan on the stovetop over medium heat for 2 minutes. Add the juice and zest from 1 lemon and the white wine and reduce by half. Taste and add more lemon juice if necessary. Reduce the heat to low and whisk in the cold butter. Do not allow the mixture to boil. Remove from the heat immediately and stir in the parsley.

Slice the veal, arrange it on a serving platter and pour the sauce overtop.

VEAL MEDALLIONS IN A TUNA AND CAPER SAUCE

Vitello Tonnato Rivisitato

VEAL MEDALLIONS

1 whole veal tenderloin,
    cleaned, tail end tucked
    under and tied
Salt
Ground black pepper
1 sprig rosemary, leaves only
Olive oil for searing
Sea salt for sprinkling

TUNA AND CAPER SAUCE

1 can tuna, packed in oil
2 anchovy fillets
4 egg yolks
¼ cup Dijon mustard
¼ cup capers
Splash of caper juice from
    the jar
¼ cup lemon juice
2 cups extra virgin olive oil
Dash Tabasco sauce
Dash Worcestershire sauce
Salt
Ground black pepper

This Italian classic is the most elegant picnic dish imaginable. Be sure to use really good-quality anchovies in this recipe, and don't be shy about using a prepared mayonnaise instead of the recipe I suggest here. This recipe is so well balanced that you won't need to add any extra salt or pepper. Trust me. **Serves 8**

Preheat the oven to 400°F.

Season the veal liberally with salt, pepper and the rosemary leaves. Brush an ovenproof pan with olive oil, heat it on the stovetop over medium-high heat and sear the veal on all sides. Transfer it to the oven and roast for 15 to 20 minutes. Remove the veal from the oven when its internal temperature reaches 130°F. Let it rest for another 10 minutes, very loosely tented in tinfoil, before slicing.

For the sauce, in a food processor combine the tuna, anchovies, egg yolks, mustard, capers, caper juice and lemon juice and process until smooth. Gradually add the olive oil in a slow and steady stream while the motor is running. Season this tuna mayonnaise with the Tabasco sauce, Worcestershire sauce, salt and pepper. If the sauce is too thick, add a little water to loosen it up.

Alternatively, you can add the tuna, anchovies, mustard, capers and caper juice, lemon juice, Tabasco sauce, Worcestershire sauce, salt and pepper to 2 cups of prepared mayonnaise.

After the veal has rested, slice it thinly. Flood the bottom of a serving platter or plate with the tuna sauce. Arrange the veal slices, slightly overlapping, on the sauce. Sprinkle a little sea salt over the meat.

This can be served cold or warm.

CORSI OSSO BUCO

Ossobuco alla Moda Mia

VEAL

6 pieces veal shank (Provimi if
  available), about 3–3½ lb in
  total, cut 1½ inches thick
Salt
Ground black pepper
1 cup all-purpose white flour
  for dredging
¼ cup olive oil
1 cup diced onion, 1-inch
  pieces
3 whole cloves of garlic, peeled
1 cup diced carrot, 1-inch
  pieces
1 cup diced celery, 1-inch
  pieces
2 cups dry red wine
4 oz chanterelle mushrooms,
  fresh or dry
1 tsp peperoncino
4 cups tomato sauce (page 15)
2 cups chicken stock
  (page 10)
Bouquet garni: fresh sage,
  rosemary, Italian parsley,
  marjoram and thyme in
  equal parts, and 1 bay leaf*

GREMOLATA

Zest of 1 lemon
1 Tbsp chopped garlic
2 Tbsp roughly chopped Italian
  parsley

* Tie the herbs in a piece of
  cheesecloth for easy removal
  when the dish is finished.

This is the Corsi family's favourite osso buco recipe. Serve this dish with espresso spoons so your guests can enjoy the bone marrow from inside the centre bone, the delicacy of the dish. The sauce is perfect with pasta the next day, but I'd be surprised if there were any leftovers.

This dish tastes even better when you make it a day ahead. Separate the meat from the sauce, cool everything quickly and refrigerate. To serve, remove the hardened fat from the top of the sauce. Reheat the veal in the sauce, adding freshly made gremolata just before serving. **Serves 6**

Lightly season the veal with salt and pepper. Tie each piece with kitchen string to hold its shape while braising then dredge in flour, shaking off any excess.

In a Dutch oven or other pot large enough to hold 18 cups of liquid, heat the oil on medium heat and brown the veal, about 4 minutes on each side. Transfer the veal to a plate. Sweat the onion and garlic in the pan until translucent, about 5 minutes. Add the carrot and celery and cook for a further 5 minutes, stirring.

Place the veal on the vegetables, add the red wine and cook for 4 minutes. Add the mushrooms and peperoncino and cook for 4 minutes. At this point you need to be careful not to break the veal. Stir gently.

Add the tomato sauce, chicken stock and bouquet garni and bring to a boil. Cover and reduce the heat to a gentle simmer. Check after 1 hour. Depending on thickness of veal it may need longer to cook. When the veal is fork-tender remove it from the heat. Discard the bouquet garni. Carefully take veal out of the sauce, remove the strings and keep it warm on a warm platter.

Skim the fat from the top of the sauce. Season to taste with more salt and pepper.

While veal is cooking, prepare the gremolata by chopping the lemon zest and mixing it with the garlic and parsley.

Stir the gremolata into the hot sauce and spoon it over the veal.

GRILLED VEAL T-BONE WITH GRANNY SMITH APPLES

Costoletta di Vitello

VEAL

2 tsp extra virgin olive oil
1 Tbsp chopped fresh thyme
1 Tbsp chopped fresh
   marjoram
Six 12 oz (or smaller) veal
   T-bone chops

SAUCE

4 Granny Smith apples,
   peeled, cored, cut into
   ½-inch wedges
2 Tbsp salted butter
1 shallot, finely diced
⅓ cup calvados or other
   apple brandy
1 cup apple juice
2 cups veal stock (page 11)

This would be a nice alternative to turkey for Thanksgiving when apples are at their peak. You could also replace the apples with pears and use pear liquor, if you prefer. **Serves 6**

Combine the oil, thyme and marjoram. Rub them into the veal and let it sit at room temperature for 1 hour before you begin cooking.

For the sauce, in a medium saucepan, sauté the apples with the butter and shallot over medium heat for 5 or 6 minutes. Flambé with the calvados (see sidebar page 160). When the flames die down, add the apple juice and reduce by three-quarters. Add the veal stock and reduce to sauce-like consistency.

While the sauce reduces, cook the veal.

Preheat the grill or a ridged pan on the stovetop on medium-high heat. Grill the veal for 4 to 5 minutes on each side for medium. The veal is ready when its internal temperature reaches 130–140°F and it's pink in the centre.

Transfer the veal to a serving platter and spoon sauce overtop.

NONNO'S MEATBALLS

Polpette di Nonno

1 loaf Italian white bread, crusts removed
2 cups whole milk
2 eggs, lightly beaten
2 lb ground beef
1½ lb ground veal
¼ lb ground lamb
2 Tbsp finely chopped garlic
2 Tbsp finely chopped Italian parsley
2 anchovy fillets, mashed with a fork to dissolve in 1 Tbsp extra virgin olive oil
4 cups tomato sauce (page 15)

After I brought my family to Canada, my father would visit us most summers. He would stay for months and delight my children and their friends with meatballs every Sunday. **Makes 48 meatballs**

Cut the bread into 1-inch cubes and soak them in the milk for 30 minutes. Remove the bread from the milk and squeeze out and discard any excess moisture. The bread should be crumbly.

In a large stainless steel bowl, combine the soaked bread, eggs, beef, veal, lamb, garlic, parsley and anchovy-oil mixture. Use your hands to mix the ingredients together well. Form them into balls, about 2 inches in diameter.

In a large saucepan, bring the tomato sauce to a boil over medium heat and add the meatballs. Reduce the heat and simmer gently until the meatballs are cooked, 30 to 45 minutes. Turn the meatballs occasionally and baste them with sauce while they're cooking.

Use half the meatballs with spaghetti for dinner. The other half can be pounded to ½-inch thickness, dusted in flour and dipped in egg and breadcrumbs, to be fried and enjoyed cold the next day for a snack.

BAROLO-MARINATED BEEF TENDERLOIN

Filetto in Marinata Cotta

BEEF

1½ lb beef tenderloin
1 cup Barolo wine, divided
1 sprig sage
1 sprig rosemary
1 clove garlic, peeled
2 cups veal stock (page 11)
1 bay leaf
Salt
Ground black pepper
2 tsp olive oil
5 oz baby arugula
¼ cup shaved Parmesan
   cheese

POLENTA CROSTINI

2 cups chicken stock
   (page 10)
2 cups whole milk
1 cup fine cornmeal
¼ cup grated Parmesan
   cheese
1 Tbsp extra virgin olive oil

This is a perfect dish for late fall. It's earthy and satisfying. I discovered a version of this recipe while visiting my friend Fiorenzo at the Batasiolo winery in Piedmont. I remember a very strong dish that used young Barolo wine to tenderize a tough piece of beef. We revisited it—*rivisitato*—as we've done with so many recipes in this book. My version is a little milder with aged Barolo and prime beef tenderloin. **Serves 6–8**

Marinate the beef tenderloin in ½ cup of the wine, the herbs and the garlic and refrigerate, covered, for at least 3 hours, and ideally overnight.

Remove the marinated beef from the fridge 1 hour before cooking. Take it out of the marinade, and strain and reserve the liquid. Pat the beef dry with paper towels.

Make the Barolo sauce by placing the strained marinating liquid, remaining ½ cup wine, veal stock and bay leaf in a medium saucepan. Cook over medium heat, reducing until the sauce thickens a little.

Preheat the oven to 350°F.

Season the beef with salt and pepper.

Heat an ovenproof pan over medium-high heat. Add the oil and, when it begins to smoke, add the beef to the pan and sear it on all sides. Transfer the pan to the oven and roast the beef until it's medium-rare (internal temperature of 130–135°F), about 15 minutes.

Rest the meat for at least 5 minutes on a cutting board before you slice it into medallions.

Meanwhile, make the polenta crostini. Line a baking sheet with Silpat or parchment paper.

Combine the stock and milk in a saucepan and bring them to a boil. Whisk in the cornmeal and cook, continuing to whisk, until thickened. Remove from the heat and add the cheese, stirring well.

Spread the mixture ¼ inch thick onto the prepared baking sheet and let it cool. You can refrigerate it until needed at this point.

Once the polenta is cool, cut it into crostini circles, about 3 inches in diameter. Heat the olive oil in a large skillet and fry both sides until they're golden brown.

Place some polenta crostini in the centre of each plate and top them with a handful of the arugula. Lay the tenderloin medallions over the arugula, drizzle with some Barolo sauce and top with the shaved Parmesan cheese.

BEEF TENDERLOIN WITH AGED BALSAMIC

Filetto Etrusca

MARINADE

1 tsp chopped fresh rosemary
1 tsp chopped fresh sage
1 tsp chopped garlic
1 tsp cayenne pepper (or
    according to taste)

BEEF

Six 6 oz pieces beef tenderloin
Oil for brushing
Salt
Ground black pepper
Aged balsamic vinegar from
    Modena to finish

Break out your best balsamic for this recipe and serve it to your favourite red-meat lover. Serve this with Wild Mushroom Ragout (page 201). **Serves 6**

Combine the marinade ingredients.

Place the beef tenderloin on a platter and sprinkle the marinade overtop. Let the beef marinate at room temperature for 1 hour before cooking.

Preheat the grill or a ridged grill pan on the stovetop to medium-high. Brush the grill surface with oil.

Season the marinated beef with salt and pepper. Grill for 5 to 6 minutes on each side for medium-rare, or to your desired doneness. Rest the beef on a cutting board for 5 minutes.

Drizzle balsamic vinegar over the beef before serving.

NEW YORK STRIP LOIN WITH GORGONZOLA

Bistecca al Gorgonzola

BEEF

Six 8 oz Alberta beef strip
   loin steaks
1 Tbsp chopped fresh sage
1 Tbsp fresh thyme leaves
Salt
Ground black pepper
6 oz gorgonzola cheese

PORT WINE *SUCCO*

½ bottle of port
2 whole cloves of garlic, peeled
2 sprigs thyme
1 bay leaf
2 cups veal stock (page 11)
Salt
Ground black pepper

Simple, satisfying and impressive. This is one of the only ways I enjoy gorgonzola cheese; this dish really mellows it out. Be sure to open a nice bottle of wine with this one. **Serves 6**

Remove the steaks from the fridge 1 hour before you're ready to begin cooking and season them with the fresh herbs and salt and pepper when you're ready to grill.

Cut the cheese into 6 portions and let it sit at room temperature.

In a saucepan on medium heat reduce the port with the garlic, thyme and bay leaf to a syrupy consistency. Add the veal stock and reduce over medium-high heat until the sauce coats the back of a spoon. Season to taste with salt and pepper. Remove the garlic cloves, thyme sprigs and bay leaf before serving.

Preheat the grill, a ridged pan on the stovetop or the broiler.

Grill the steaks to your liking, top each with a piece of gorgonzola and broil until the cheese has melted.

Place the steaks on warm plates surrounded by port wine *succo*.

EDITH'S STUFFED RED BELL PEPPERS
Peperoni Ripieni alla Edith

6 large red bell peppers
1 Tbsp extra virgin olive oil
¼ cup diced onion
1 lb lean ground beef
Salt
Ground black pepper
1 cup dry red wine
1 cup cooked risotto (page 21)
2 cups tomato sauce
(page 15), divided
2 Tbsp chopped fresh oregano
or 1 tsp dried
2 Tbsp chopped fresh Italian
parsley
¼ cup grated Parmesan

This is one of my wife's specialties, and it's my daughter Ida's favourite. **Serves 6**

Slice the tops off the peppers and reserve. Remove the seeds and ribs from inside and discard. Blanch the peppers in salted boiling water for 5 minutes, then remove and cool.

Preheat the oven to 375°F. Lightly grease a baking dish large enough to hold all the peppers without crowding.

Heat the oil in a skillet over medium heat and sauté the onion for 2 to 3 minutes. Increase the heat to high, add the ground beef, sprinkle with salt and pepper, and cook for 5 minutes.

Add the red wine and reduce until it's almost dry. Stir in the risotto, ½ cup of the tomato sauce, the oregano and the parsley. Combine everything well and remove the pan from the heat. Add the Parmesan cheese and season to taste with more salt and pepper.

Divide the stuffing evenly between the peppers and replace their tops. Place the peppers in the prepared dish and cover. Bake for 40 minutes.

In a small saucepan, heat the remaining tomato sauce and serve it over the cooked bell peppers.

ROAST BEEF WITH ROSEMARY POTATOES
Arrosto di Manzo

2 Tbsp extra virgin olive oil, divided
4 lb top sirloin roast of beef
4 cloves garlic, peeled
1 Tbsp finely chopped fresh rosemary, divided
2 Tbsp coarse salt
1 tsp coarsely ground black pepper
2 lb German butter potatoes,* split in half, about 2-inch pieces
Salt
½ cup dry red wine
½ cup veal demi-glace (page 11)

* Small Yukon Gold or other buttery potatoes may be substituted.

Although not the usual Sunday night dinner in Italy, roast beef is popular at weddings and larger family celebrations there. I like serving it to my growing family when all I want to do is put something in the oven and let it cook itself. **Serves 8 (or more)**

Preheat the oven to 400°F.

Rub 1 Tbsp of the olive oil all over the beef roast. Make 4 small slashes in the top of the roast and push a garlic clove into each one.

Mix together half the rosemary, the salt and the pepper and roll the roast in this seasoning. Place the roast in a roasting pan and roast for 30 minutes. Reduce the oven temperature to 350°F and roast for another hour. Do not baste the meat as it roasts.

In a bowl, toss the potatoes with remaining rosemary and 1 Tbsp olive oil, lightly salt them and add them to the roasting pan. Cook the potatoes with the meat for 1 hour then check for doneness. Allow the meat to rest for 20 minutes on a carving board. Transfer the potatoes to an ovenproof bowl and keep them warm in the turned-off oven.

Place the roasting pan on the stovetop over medium heat and deglaze it with the red wine, reducing it by half. Add the demi-glace and reduce to a sauce consistency.

Slice the beef and arrange on a warm platter with the roasted potatoes. Pass the sauce at the table.

SAUSAGE AND BEANS
Salsicce con Fagioli

12 spicy Italian sausages
3 Tbsp extra virgin olive oil,
  if required
6 Roma tomatoes, peeled,
  seeded, cut in ½-inch dice
  (1½ cups tomato concasse)
Two 14 oz cans cannellini
  beans, rinsed and drained
Salt
Ground black pepper

There's soul food and then there's show-off food. Guess which category this fits into?
Serves 6–8

Use a skewer to poke holes in the Italian sausages and place them in a large sauté pan with a lid. Add enough cold water to cover the sausages and bring it to a boil. Reduce the heat, cover and simmer gently. Cook, turning the sausages from time to time, until the water has evaporated. Remove the sausages from the pan and keep them warm.

If there's no fat left in the pan, add the extra virgin olive oil. Stir in the tomato concasse and sauté for 10 minutes over medium heat. Add the drained cannellini beans and cook for 10 minutes, or until the sauce thickens. Return the sausages to the pan and heat them through. Season to taste with salt and pepper.

TRIPE WITH PANCETTA

Trippa alla Maenzana

¼ lb pancetta, cut in
  ½-inch dice
1 onion, cut in ½-inch dice
¼ cup extra virgin olive oil
2 Tbsp finely chopped garlic
4 stalks celery, cut in ½-inch
  dice
1 carrot, cut in ½-inch dice
1 Tbsp peperoncino
1 cup dry white wine
3 lb pre-cooked tripe, cut in
  1- × 3-inch strips
4 cups chicken stock (page 10)
4 cups tomato sauce (page 15)
1 Tbsp chopped fresh mint
½ cup grated pecorino Romano

I'll admit that tripe is not for everyone. Either you love it, or you can't stomach the idea of it, if you'll pardon the pun. I love this delicacy, of course, and this is my favourite way to enjoy it. Be sure to purchase your tripe from a trusted source. **Serves 6**

In a pot with a lid, sauté the pancetta and onion in the extra virgin olive oil until the pancetta is crisp. Add the garlic and sauté for 1 minute. Add the celery and carrot and sauté for 5 minutes.

Add the peperoncino and white wine. Reduce the volume by half before adding the tripe.

Combine the chicken stock and tomato sauce together in a separate container. Slowly add the chicken stock and tomato to the tripe mixture. Bring to a boil, reduce the heat and cover. Simmer gently over low heat for 20 to 30 minutes until the tripe is tender and the sauce is slightly thick. Finish with fresh mint and pecorino Romano.

Serve warm.

VEGETABLES

Verdure

RAPINI TIMBALES WITH MORTADELLA

Sformatini di Rapini con Mortadella

SAUCE

4 onions

3 carrots, peeled

3 stalks celery

8 cups water

4–5 parsley stems (no leaves)

2 bay leaves

1 leek, well washed

Salt

Ground black pepper

TIMBALES

1 bunch rapini

1 Tbsp butter, divided

1 Tbsp + 2 tsp chopped garlic

Pinch chili flakes

1½ cups whipping cream

2 eggs

2 Tbsp shaved Parmesan
cheese

2 Tbsp sliced almonds

Pinch grated nutmeg

Salt

Pinch ground black pepper

4 oz mortadella sausage, cut
in julienne strips

I love mortadella. Everyone else in my household likes ham and turkey, so I'm the only one who eats it at home. One day I was having some of Edith's leftover broccoli for lunch (page 190) with my favourite deli meat, and the combination was great. I developed this recipe using rapini instead of broccoli. Sometimes your palate talks to you and you just have to listen. **Serves 6**

For the sauce, take 3 of the onions, 2 of the carrots and 2 stalks of the celery and roughly chop them. Place them in a stockpot and add the 8 cups water, parsley and bay leaves. Bring to a boil on medium-high heat, reduce the heat to low and simmer for 45 minutes. Strain this stock through a fine-mesh sieve into a clean saucepan and discard the solids.

Finely dice the remaining onion, carrot and celery plus the leek. Add them to the stock and cook on medium heat for 20 to 30 minutes, reducing slowly to about 10 percent. Season to taste with salt and pepper.

Preheat the oven to 350°F. Grease 6 ramekins, each about 3¼ inches across and 2 inches deep. Line the bottom of each ramekin with parchment, then butter the paper.

For the timbales, bring a large pot of salted water to a boil on high heat. Blanch the rapini until tender, 3 to 4 minutes, then drain.

Heat 2 tsp of the butter in a skillet on medium heat. Sauté the blanched rapini, garlic and chili flakes for 5 minutes, until the moisture evaporates. Transfer the rapini to a bowl. Let it cool then purée it in a food processor until it's fairly smooth.

In a bowl, whisk together the puréed rapini, cream, eggs, Parmesan cheese, almonds, nutmeg, salt to taste and the pinch of pepper. Fill the ramekins three-quarters full with this custard mixture.

Set the ramekins in a large roasting pan and add just enough hot water to reach halfway up the sides of the dishes. Bake for 30 minutes, until the custard is just set. Gently shake the ramekins, and if the custard jiggles slightly it's done. Remove the roasting pan from the oven and transfer the ramekins to a rack.

(continued on page 188)

RAPINI TIMBALES WITH MORTADELLA (CONT'D)

While the timbales are cooking, heat the remaining butter in a skillet on medium heat. Sauté the mortadella until it's crispy. Use a slotted spoon to transfer it to paper towels to absorb any excess oil.

To serve, reheat the sauce on the stovetop and reheat the ramekins in a 350°F oven for a few minutes (you don't need the water bath this time). Run a knife around the edge of each ramekin. Place a plate over the top of each ramekin then invert both the ramekin and the plate. Unmould the timbales then remove the parchment paper.

Garnish the timbales with the crispy mortadella and drizzle with sauce.

Serve with mixed greens.

CANNELLINI BEANS SILVANA

Fagioli alla Silvana

¼ cup extra virgin olive oil
½ lb chicken livers, chopped
3 anchovy fillets, chopped
¼ cup diced onion
¼ cup cubed Genoa salami,
　½-inch pieces
¼ cup diced pancetta, ½-inch
　pieces
1 Tbsp finely chopped garlic
½ cup red wine vinegar
1 tsp granulated sugar
Pinch nutmeg
Two 14 oz cans cannellini
　beans, drained, rinsed,
　liquid reserved
Salt
Ground black pepper
2 Tbsp chopped Italian parsley

This recipe comes from our very dear family friend Silvana. This is actually her grandmother's recipe. **Serves 6**

Heat the olive oil in a large skillet over medium heat and sauté the chicken livers, anchovies, onion, salami, pancetta and garlic for 8 to 10 minutes, until the liver is cooked and the pancetta is crisp.

Deglaze the pan with the red wine vinegar, scraping up the brown bits from the bottom of the pan. Stir in the sugar and nutmeg and continue cooking for 3 to 4 minutes.

Add the cannellini beans with half their reserved liquid and cook until they've warmed through.

Season to taste with salt and pepper and sprinkle with fresh Italian parsley.

EDITH'S BROCCOLI

Broccoli Stracotti

2 heads broccoli, crowns only
½ cup extra virgin olive oil
2 whole cloves of garlic
1 Tbsp peperoncino chili flakes
Salt
Ground black pepper

This is on the table every Sunday night. Patrick and Ida come home just for Mom's mushy broccoli. **Serves 6**

Cook the broccoli crowns in boiling salted water for 10 to 15 minutes. Drain and roughly chop it.

Heat the oil on medium heat in a large skillet and lightly brown the garlic cloves for 2 minutes. Remove and discard the garlic. Add the chopped broccoli and peperoncino, stirring frequently with a wooden spoon until it's well done, about 10 minutes. Season to taste with salt and pepper.

You can also use rapini for this recipe. The cooking time will be about 5 minutes longer than it is for broccoli.

ZUCCHINI IN VINEGAR

Zucchine all' Aceto

6 zucchinis, sliced ¾ inch
   thick
½ cup extra virgin olive oil
Salt
Ground black pepper
¼ cup white wine vinegar
2 Tbsp chopped Italian parsley
1 Tbsp chopped garlic

This zesty combination is perfect with seafood dishes like Spot Prawns in Vermouth Sauce (page 140). Get the zucchini fresh from the garden and the prawns straight from the dock. **Serves 6**

In a large skillet over medium-high heat, fry the zucchini in the olive oil until it's light golden brown. Season with salt and pepper to taste. Transfer the zucchini with its cooking oil to a bowl and add the vinegar, parsley and garlic. Toss everything together and let stand at room temperature for 1 hour before serving.

   Before serving, you may wish to add more vinegar to taste.

GREEN BEANS WITH TOMATO

Fagiolini al Tegame

¼ cup extra virgin olive oil

1 onion, cut in julienne strips

4 Roma tomatoes, peeled, seeded, cut in ½-inch dice (1 cup tomato concasse)

2 lb green beans, washed, tips removed

Salt

Ground black pepper

My brother Claudio in Italy serves this dish with everything. I can guarantee that it will be on the table at his house. I like this alongside Cornish game hen. **Serves 6**

Heat the olive oil in a sauté pan over medium heat. Add the onion and sweat it for 2 to 3 minutes. Add the tomato concasse and sweat it for another 7 to 8 minutes. Add the beans, and salt and pepper to taste. Cover the pan with a lid, reduce the heat to a simmer and cook slowly until the beans are tender.

If the moisture in pan evaporates before the beans are cooked, add some water to finish them off.

Serve warm.

CHEESE RAPINI

Rapini Farciti

4 bunches rapini, about 1 lb
  each, well washed
4 anchovy fillets, finely
  chopped
½ lb grated caciocavallo
  cheese
1 onion, cut in julienne strips
1 cup chopped black olives
½ cup olive oil, divided + extra
  for oiling
¾ cup dry red wine

This recipe is everything that's great about rapini. It's salty and bitter and incredibly good. This just may become your new favourite vegetable side dish. **Serves 6–8**

Cut the rapini in 4-inch pieces. Remove the fibrous part of the stems and any tough outer leaves.

In a stainless steel bowl, mix together the anchovies, cheese, onion, olives and ¼ cup of the olive oil.

Preheat the oven to 350°F. Lightly grease an ovenproof 9- × 13-inch pan with olive oil.

Add one-third of the rapini to the prepared pan and press it down. Top with a layer of the olive mixture, followed by a layer of rapini, another layer of olive mixture and a final layer of rapini. Press down between each addition.

Pour the red wine and remaining ¼ cup olive oil overtop, cover and bake for 40 minutes, or until the rapini is soft and cooked.

This can be served hot or cold.

EGGPLANT WITH FONTINA CHEESE

Melanzane al Pomodoro

2 large eggplants
Salt
½ cup extra virgin olive oil,
  divided
12 slices fontina cheese,
  ¼ inch thick
4 eggs
1 Tbsp yellow mustard seeds
2 cups warm tomato sauce
  (page 15)

This is eggplant parmigiana all'Antonio. It's ideal alongside veal or chicken. **Makes 12 stacks**

Line a baking sheet with paper towel.

Slice each eggplant crosswise into 12 pieces, ½ inch thick. Lay the slices on the paper towel and lightly salt them. Leave them for 30 minutes to 1 hour then wipe off any excess moisture.

Heat ¼ cup of the olive oil over medium-high heat in a large non-stick skillet. When the oil is very hot fry the eggplant slices until they're softened and golden brown on both sides, about 2 minutes per side. You'll probably need 2 to 3 Tbsp more oil to complete the frying.

Remove the eggplant slices from the pan and sandwich a piece of fontina between 2 slices of eggplant to make 12 stacks.

In a bowl, whisk the eggs with the mustard seeds.

Reheat the pan over medium heat, adding 1 Tbsp oil. Dip the eggplant stacks in the egg mixture and fry them until they're golden brown and the cheese has melted.

Serve warm over the tomato sauce.

EGGPLANT BOATS

Melanzane in Barca

3 medium or large eggplants
4 anchovy fillets, chopped
½ cup breadcrumbs
½ cup pitted, chopped black
  olives
¼ cup extra virgin olive oil
  + extra for brushing on
  eggplant
3 Tbsp whole capers
2 Tbsp chopped Italian parsley
2 Tbsp chopped fresh oregano
4 Roma tomatoes, peeled,
  seeded, cut in ½-inch dice
  (1 cup tomato concasse)
6 slices fresh mozzarella
6 tsp salted butter
¼ cup toasted pine nuts

This is one of my lunch favourites. **Serves 6**

Preheat the oven to 350°F.

Slice off and discard the stem ends of the eggplants and cut them in half lengthwise. Scoop out the flesh, leaving a ½-inch wall all around. If the halves don't sit flat take a very thin slice off the bottom, keeping flesh intact. Chop the eggplant flesh into ¾-inch cubes.

In a mixing bowl combine the eggplant cubes, anchovy fillets, breadcrumbs, olives, olive oil, capers, parsley and oregano.

Brush the eggplant boats with oil and lightly salt the insides. Fill the boats with the eggplant-anchovy mix. Top each boat evenly with tomato concasse, place them on a rimmed baking sheet and roast for 45 minutes to 1 hour. When the eggplants are soft remove them from the oven.

Top each eggplant boat with a slice of mozzarella and 1 tsp salted butter. Return them to the oven until the cheese is melted and the butter is golden brown.

Transfer the boats onto a large platter and scatter with toasted pine nuts.

FENNEL IN GARLIC
Finocchio all' Aglio

3 bulbs medium-sized fennel
3 Tbsp extra virgin olive oil
1 Tbsp finely chopped garlic
2 cups water
Salt
Ground black pepper

This is very nice with a piquant dish like Veal Scaloppine with Vodka (page 167). **Serves 6**

Cut the stalks off the top of each fennel bulb, discard a thin slice from the bottom and cut each bulb into 6 wedges.

In a large skillet with a lid, sauté the fennel pieces in the olive oil over medium heat until they're light gold on all sides, 4 to 5 minutes. Add the garlic and sauté for 1 minute. Cover with the 2 cups water, and salt and pepper to taste. Place the lid on the pan and cook until the fennel is fork-tender, 10 to 12 minutes. Check the water level occasionally and add more if it's very low.

POTATOES IN PARCHMENT

Patate Affumicate

18 new potatoes, about
   1½ inches in diameter,
   left whole
2 Tbsp Dijon mustard
18 slices smoked pancetta
2 Tbsp olive oil
½ lb fresh porcini or cremini
   mushrooms, left whole,
   or halved or quartered,
   depending on size
2 cloves garlic, crushed
2 bay leaves
Salt
Ground black pepper

Now this is a roasted potato! This produces a lovely smoky flavour, and is almost a meal in itself. **Serves 6**

Parboil the potatoes for 5 minutes then dry them. Coat them with the Dijon mustard then wrap them in the pancetta. Use your hands to stick the pancetta to the potatoes then secure it with a toothpick.

Heat the olive oil in a large sauté pan over medium heat. Brown the wrapped potatoes until they're crisp. Remove them from the heat and reserve. Add the mushrooms to the pan and cook them for 2 minutes, or until they're beginning to soften.

Preheat the oven to 375°F.

Place the parchment paper on a clean work surface and add the reserved potatoes in 1 layer. Top them with the softened mushrooms, garlic, bay leaves and a little salt and pepper. Bring the sides up to meet, roll them down snugly, then fold the ends under, creasing the paper firmly to seal the package. Place the package on a rimmed baking sheet and bake for 15 to 20 minutes.

BAKED MUSHROOMS
Funghi al Forno

6 large portobello mushrooms
2 anchovy fillets, finely
 chopped
½ cup fresh breadcrumbs
½ cup grated pecorino
 Romano
¼ cup extra virgin olive oil
2 Tbsp chopped chives
1 Tbsp chopped fresh mint
1 Tbsp finely chopped garlic
Salt
Ground black pepper

I make these all the time. By now the anchovies will be no surprise to you. The mint gives the spark and lightness to this recipe. If you're serving vegetarians, simply omit the anchovies in this recipe. **Serves 6**

Preheat the oven to 400°F.

Take the stems and gills from the portobello mushrooms (reserving the caps), chop them finely and place them in a bowl.

Add the anchovies, breadcrumbs, cheese, oil, chives, mint, garlic and salt and pepper to the chopped mushrooms. Combine everything well and stuff the mixture evenly into the mushroom caps.

Wrap each cap in tinfoil and bake for 20 to 25 minutes.

Remove from the foil before serving. Serve hot!

WILD MUSHROOM RAGOUT

Ragú ai Funghi

1 oz dry porcini mushrooms
1 cup warm water
2 shallots, finely diced
1 Tbsp finely chopped garlic
2 tsp salted butter
2 oz fresh chanterelle
   mushrooms, thinly sliced
2 portobello mushrooms,
   stems discarded, thinly
   sliced
⅓ cup brandy
1 cup veal stock (page 11)
Salt
Ground black pepper

This sauce plus a loaf of rustic Italian bread, and a glass of Chianti, equals heaven.
Makes 1¼ cups

Soak the porcini mushrooms in the warm water for 30 minutes.

In a skillet over medium-high heat sauté the shallots and garlic in the butter for 2 minutes.

Strain the porcini mushrooms through a fine-mesh sieve, saving the liquid. Pick over the mushrooms, discarding any grit, chop them and add them to the shallot mixture with the chanterelles and portobellos. Sauté for 6 to 8 minutes until the mushrooms absorb their liquid. Flambé with the brandy and wait until the flame goes out (see sidebar page 160). Add the reserved porcini mushroom liquid and reduce by half. Add the veal stock and reduce until lightly syrupy.

Season to taste with salt and pepper.

DESSERTS

Dolci

PHYLLO, SOUR CHERRY AND MASCARPONE TOWERS
Ciliege Filate

PHYLLO LAYERS

4 sheets phyllo pastry, taken
    from freezer about 1 hour
    before cooking
⅓ cup unsalted butter, melted
1⅓ cups icing sugar

CHERRY COMPOTE

2 cups frozen sour cherries,
    thawed*
½ cup dried sour cherries
¾ cup sugar
1 cup red wine, divided
1 Tbsp cornstarch

MASCARPONE CREAM

1 vanilla bean
1 cup whipping cream
1 cup mascarpone cheese
⅓ cup icing sugar

*If frozen cherries aren't
    available, use fresh and
    reduce the red wine to
    ¾ cup.

This is quite simply a Quattro classic: crispy phyllo, rich mascarpone and a gorgeous sour cherry and red wine compote. *Perfetto!* **Serves 6**

Begin with the phyllo layers.

Preheat the oven to 375°F.

Gently unroll the phyllo and remove 4 sheets. Place them on a clean work surface under a piece of plastic wrap to keep them from drying out. Return the rest of the phyllo to the freezer.

Place 1 sheet of phyllo on a piece of parchment paper. Brush it all over with about one-quarter of the melted butter then sift about ⅓ cup of the icing sugar generously over the surface. Top with a second sheet of phyllo. Brush this with butter and dust it with another ⅓ cup icing sugar. Repeat with the last 2 sheets, covering the top sheet with butter and icing sugar as you did with the others.

Using a pizza wheel or sharp knife, trim the edges of the phyllo to create a clean rectangle. Cut this into 3-inch squares, which will give you about 20 squares, depending on the size of the phyllo you're using.

Cover the phyllo squares with a second piece of parchment paper. Gently slide the squares and parchment onto a baking tray. Check that the phyllo has not shifted, then place a second baking tray on top of the first so that the phyllo is tightly sandwiched.

Bake the phyllo until it's a deep golden colour, about 10 minutes. Be extremely careful when you lift the hot trays to check on it. Remove the phyllo from the oven, remove the top tray and set aside.

Before the phyllo has cooled completely, use the pizza wheel or sharp knife to reinforce the edges of the squares where the sugar may have melted. This will help you separate the squares without breaking them when they're cool.

When cool, remove the phyllo squares from the tray and transfer them to an airtight container for up to 3 days until you're ready to use them.

For the cherry compote, place the thawed sour cherries, dried sour cherries, sugar and all but 3 Tbsp of the red wine in a saucepan. Simmer these over medium heat until the sugar dissolves.

(continued on page 206)

PHYLLO, SOUR CHERRY AND MASCARPONE TOWERS (CONT'D)

Mix the cornstarch and reserved 3 Tbsp red wine together in a small bowl until no lumps remain. Add this to the cherries and stir until the mixture begins to thicken, about 10 minutes.

Remove the cherries from the heat, transfer them to a container and chill in the fridge.

For the mascarpone cream, slice the vanilla bean lengthwise and scrape the seeds into the cream. Whip the cream, mascarpone and icing sugar until the mixture thickens and forms soft peaks. Refrigerate the cream until you're ready to use it, or until the use-by date on the container.

Assemble the towers just before serving. Allow 3 phyllo squares for each plate.

Place a square of phyllo on each plate. Top it with a dollop of mascarpone cream and a spoonful of cherry compote. Add a second phyllo square, more cream and more cherries to the first. Finish with a third square topped with cream and drizzle the last spoonful of cherry compote decoratively on top and around the stack.

BANANA RASPBERRY SUNDAE

Banana con Lamponi

BANANAS
6 bananas
3 cups medium-dry white wine
1 cup granulated sugar

ALMOND BRITTLE
3 Tbsp butter
1 cup almonds, sliced,
   blanched
¼ cup granulated sugar
¼ cup Grand Marnier

TOPPING
Vanilla or banana ice cream
1½ cups fresh raspberries
2 Tbsp icing sugar

This is not your everyday sundae. **Serves 6**

Slice the bananas on an angle.

Combine the white wine with the 1 cup sugar in a saucepan, bring it to a boil and immediately add the bananas. Poach the bananas for about 4 minutes. They'll soften, but will maintain their shape.

For the almond brittle, in a separate pan, melt the butter and sauté the almonds for about 3 minutes. Add the ¼ cup sugar, stirring constantly with a wooden spoon, until the mixture is golden brown. Add the Grand Marnier and quickly flambé (see sidebar page 160).

Pour the almond mixture onto a baking tray and let it cool. Once it has cooled, crumble it into small pieces.

To serve, place a scoop of the ice cream at the centre of a dessert plate. Surround the ice cream with a ring of the raspberries then surround the raspberries with a ring of the poached bananas. Sprinkle the crumbled almond brittle and icing sugar overtop.

PISTACHIO SHORTCAKE

Fragole al Pistacchio

PISTACHIO FRANGIPANE

1¼ cups pistachios, shelled
¾ cup + 2 Tbsp butter
4 oz marzipan
2 cups icing sugar + more for
    dusting
1 vanilla bean
2 tsp pure vanilla extract
4 eggs
⅔ cup all-purpose white flour
⅛ tsp salt

STRAWBERRY FILLING

1 cup diced strawberries
    (size of raisins)
3 Tbsp granulated sugar
Juice of 1 lemon

WHIPPED CREAM

2 cups whipping cream
3 Tbsp icing sugar

This dessert is absolutely gorgeous on a summer's day—green pistachio frangipane sandwiching red strawberries and velvety whipped cream. Magnifico! **Serves 6**

Begin with the pistachio frangipane.

Preheat the oven to 375°F. Line a 9- × 5-inch loaf pan or an 8-inch square cake pan with parchment paper. Alternatively, grease it well. If you choose to grease, you must let the cake cool completely before unmoulding it very gently.

Grind the pistachios in a food processor, using a pulse action to avoid making pistachio butter. A mix of finely ground and coarser nuts gives this frangipane great texture.

In a stand mixer, or using handheld beaters in a large bowl, beat the butter and marzipan until they combine to form a smooth paste. Add the icing sugar and beat the mixture until it lightens.

Use a paring knife to slit the vanilla bean lengthwise then scrape the seeds into the butter mixture. Add the vanilla extract and beat to combine. Beat in the ground pistachios. Add the eggs, 1 at a time, scraping well between additions. Add the flour and salt and beat for 1 minute to lighten the batter.

Scrape the batter into the prepared pan and smooth the top with an offset spatula or the back of a spoon to spread it evenly into all the corners.

Bake until the frangipane turns a deep golden brown, about 45 minutes, rotating the pan a quarter turn about every 15 minutes while it bakes. The cake is done when it has a crusty edge and is a deep golden brown. The inside of this cake is super moist and the top and bottom develop a delicious, caramel crust. At the restaurant when the pastry chef makes this cake, the staff clamours to eat the dark, crackly edges that aren't used!

Remove the frangipane from the oven and cool it in the pan on a rack until it's firm enough to be gently removed. You can pull gently on the parchment paper edges to lift it out of the pan for minimal cracking. Don't leave it in its pan too long, or the moisture from the hot metal will soften the crust too much.

While the cake is cooling, toss the strawberries with the sugar and lemon juice in a bowl. Marinate them for 15 minutes.

Strain the strawberries for several minutes through a fine-mesh sieve set over a bowl to catch the juice. Reserve the strawberries and their juice separately.

Whip the cream with the icing sugar to form soft peaks. This can rest in the fridge until you're ready to use it.

When you're ready to serve, cut the crisp edges from the frangipane and slice the cake into 6 equal squares. Cut each square in half horizontally, to create a cake "sandwich."

Place each bottom cake square on a plate. Top them each with a dollop of whipped cream and a generous spoonful of berries. Gently press each top cake square on top to create shortcakes. Dust with more icing sugar and drizzle with a little of the reserved strawberry juice before serving.

RED WINE SORBET WITH HONEY TUILES

Sorbetto al Vino Rosso

RED WINE SORBET

3 cups red wine, a fruity young
    merlot would be suitable
1½ cups granulated sugar
3 Tbsp liquid honey
1½ cups water
2 lemons
2 small oranges
1 Tbsp cassis (black currant
    liqueur or similar)

HONEY TUILES

¼ cup granulated sugar
¼ cup liquid honey
3 egg whites
¾ cup all-purpose white flour
1 tsp cornstarch
¼ cup + 2 Tbsp butter, melted

Fruity red wine sorbet served with a crisp honey tuile. What could be simpler or more perfect? You'll need a tabletop ice cream maker for this recipe, but in a pinch you could substitute a rectangular metal pan and fork for a great granita! **Serves 6**

For the red wine sorbet, place the red wine, sugar, honey and water in a saucepan. Slice the lemons and oranges in half and add them to the saucepan. Bring the ingredients to a boil over medium heat, and stir until the sugar is dissolved.

Strain the sorbet base through a fine-mesh sieve, then add the cassis. Chill this in the fridge, or until it's cold.

Freeze the sorbet base in an ice cream maker, following the manufacturer's instructions.

If you don't have an ice cream maker, pour the sorbet base into a rectangular metal pan and place it in the freezer. Stir it every 20 minutes with a fork until the mixture is frozen, about 1½ to 2 hours. It will look flaky and granular when it's ready.

Meanwhile, make the honey tuiles.

Preheat the oven to 325°F. Line a baking sheet with parchment paper or oil it well.

Beat the sugar, honey and egg whites until the mixture begins to lighten, about 1 minute. Add the flour and cornstarch. Mix to combine. Slowly add the melted butter, mixing to form a smooth, shiny batter.

Spoon about 1 Tbsp of the batter for each tuile onto the prepared baking sheet. Using a small offset spatula or the back of a spoon, spread the tuile batter into thin (about ⅛ inch), rectangular shapes about the size of 2 fingers (roughly 4 × 1½ inches).

Bake the tuiles until they're golden all over, 10 to 12 minutes, giving the tray a 180 degree turn once during baking. Cool the tuiles on the tray, then gently transfer them to an airtight container for up to 2 days until you're ready to use them.

To serve, scoop the sorbet into bowls and decorate each bowl with a tuile. Serve extra tuiles on the side.

VANILLA BEAN PANNACOTTA WITH FRESH BERRIES

Pannacotta alla Vaniglia

2 vanilla beans
1¾ cups whipping cream
   (the freshest, best quality
   you can get)
3 Tbsp liquid honey
1 Tbsp + 1 tsp granulated
   sugar
1¾ tsp powdered gelatin
1 Tbsp water

This recipe is fabulous on a warm summer evening with a glass of sweet white wine. Start the recipe early in the day, or the day before serving. **Serves 6**

Use a paring knife to slit the vanilla beans lengthwise then scrape the seeds and pod into a pot. Add the cream, honey and sugar and bring to a boil over medium heat. Remove the pot from heat, cover and set aside to allow the ingredients to steep.

Sprinkle the gelatin over the water and let it soften for 3 minutes. Whisk one-quarter of the warm cream mixture into the gelatin, transfer this to the pot and stir over low heat to dissolve completely.

Strain the pannacotta mixture through a fine-meshed sieve into a pitcher, and divide it between six ⅓-cup ramekins.

Chill the pannacottas in the fridge, covered, until they've set, 6 hours or overnight.

To serve, dip the bottom of the ramekins into hot water for 30 seconds. Run a paring knife around the edge of each then gently invert them onto a serving platter. You may need to shake the ramekins lightly to loosen them.

Serve the pannacottas with a variety of berries (blackberries, blueberries, raspberries, strawberries), spread decoratively around each plate.

Instead of using ramekins you can pour the pannacotta mixture into wine or martini glasses. Serve these topped with berries.

CHESTNUT MOUSSE

Castagnaccio

2 cups chestnut purée
   (unsweetened)
2 cups granulated sugar
½ cup ricotta cheese
4 sheets gelatin, or ¼ oz
   (1 packet) powdered gelatin
   + 2 Tbsp cold water
2 Tbsp amaretto liqueur
1 cup whipping cream,
   whipped to medium peaks

This is a very elegant dessert for the not-too-sweet set. **Serves 8**

Purée the chestnut purée, sugar and ricotta until smooth. A food processor is ideal for this but you could push everything through a fine-mesh sieve and beat until smooth.

If you're using sheet gelatin, soak the individual sheets in water according to the package instructions. Squeeze out any excess water and heat them gently with the amaretto until they've dissolved.

If you're using powdered gelatin, sprinkle it with 2 Tbsp cold water. Let it soften for 3 minutes then heat it gently with the amaretto until it's dissolved.

Whisk a little chestnut-ricotta purée into the gelatin mixture to cool it down then stir it all into the chestnut-ricotta purée. Gently fold in the whipped cream and transfer it to the fridge for at least 4 hours to set.

Pipe the mousse into Almond Lace Cookies (page 220) or serve it with crumbled Crunchy Amaretti cookies (page 221).

CRÈME CARAMEL

Crema Caramellata

CARAMEL

1 cup granulated sugar
¼ cup water

CRÈME

2 cups whipping cream
½ cup granulated sugar
1 vanilla bean, slit and
    seeds scraped
6 egg yolks

Watch out! This just may be the richest crème caramel ever. When I first came to Canada I would often order two or three of these pannacotta-like desserts at a time in a restaurant. I just can't get enough of the burnt caramel flavour. **Serves 4 or 8, according to ramekin size**

For the caramel, have four 6 oz (or eight 3 oz) ovenproof ramekins at hand.

    Measure the sugar and water into a small pot and bring them to a boil. Do not stir. Once the mixture is boiling, reduce the heat and, watching carefully, swirl the pan around almost constantly. The mixture will appear cloudy at first, but it will clear and bubble. When the sugar is a deep brown colour, divide it evenly between the ramekins, coating the bottom only. Place the ramekins in a deep-sided baking pan. Let the caramel sit and harden. Once the caramel has hardened, prepare the crème.

    Preheat the oven to 325°F.

    Heat the cream with the sugar and vanilla bean in a saucepan.

    Beat the egg yolks in a separate bowl and very gradually drizzle in the hot cream mixture, whisking constantly. Strain the custard and pour it into the caramel-lined ramekins. Pour hot water in the baking pan to halfway up the sides of the ramekins and bake for about 30 minutes. The custards should jiggle slightly in the centre when they're done. Chill for at least 6 hours or overnight.

    To serve, run a knife blade around the edge of the custard in the ramekin and invert it onto a plate.

    Serve with Crunchy Amaretti cookies (page 221) and fresh fruit.

QUATTRO TIRAMISU

Tiramisù al Modo Nostro

⅔ cup whipping cream
1 lb tub mascarpone cheese
1½ tsp powdered gelatin
1 Tbsp water
½ cup granulated sugar
7 egg yolks
2 Tbsp orange-flavoured
  liqueur, like Grand Marnier
  or Cointreau
1 cup espresso or strong
  coffee, cooled
¼ cup Kahlúa
14 oz package ladyfingers
  (Savoiardi)*
Grated chocolate or cocoa
  powder

* Available at specialty
  markets or your local Italian
  deli. Look for Savoiardi
  made from just eggs, sugar
  and flour—they have the
  best flavour.

The classic velvety smooth dessert, fragrant from the coffee and liqueur. This version is light and airy. **Makes one 8-inch-square cake, serves 6–9**

Whip the cream to medium peaks and set it aside.

Place the mascarpone in a separate bowl, and use a spatula to smooth and soften it. Set this aside.

Sprinkle the gelatin over the water in a small bowl and let it soften for 3 minutes.

In another bowl, whisk the sugar into the yolks, set them over a simmering pot of water and whisk vigorously until very thick, light and pale.

Place the bowl with the gelatin over a pot of simmering water, and stir gently to melt the gelatin. Add a small amount of the yolk mixture to the gelatin to temper it, then whisk the gelatin into the yolks.

Add the softened mascarpone to the yolk mixture and whisk this until everything is thoroughly incorporated with no lumps. Stir in the orange liqueur then gently fold in the whipped cream. Set this aside.

Combine the espresso with the Kahlúa. Dip each ladyfinger quickly into the espresso-Kahlúa mix and tuck it snugly into the bottom of an 8-inch-square cake pan. (Soak the ladyfingers just to flavour and soften them, but not so much that they disintegrate, about 1 full second per dip.) Continue until the bottom of the pan is covered.

Pour half the mascarpone mixture over the ladyfingers. Tap the pan on the counter to distribute it evenly. Continue dipping the remaining ladyfingers to cover the first layer of mascarpone. Freeze any leftover ladyfingers to keep them fresh.

Cover the second layer of ladyfingers with the remaining mascarpone mixture and refrigerate for several hours or overnight, until set.

Grate the dark chocolate over the surface of the tiramisu, or dust it with cocoa powder. Cut it into 6 to 9 portions and serve with strong coffee!

MILK CHOCOLATE SEMIFREDDO WITH TOASTED ALMONDS

Semifreddo alla Mandorla

1 cup whole, natural almonds
1 cup whipping cream
1¼ cups chopped milk
   chocolate (about 6 oz)
1 egg
2 egg yolks
2 Tbsp liquid honey
2 tsp dark rum

This velvety semifreddo contrasts richly with the flavour of the toasted nuts. A flexible silicone mould with individual pockets (a muffin mould, for example) is ideal for this recipe. **Serves 6**

Preheat the oven to 350°F.

Spread the almonds on a rimmed baking sheet and toast in the oven until the inside nutmeat turns the colour of light toffee, 10 to 12 minutes. Remove them from the oven and cool. Coarsely chop the almonds and store them in an airtight container.

Whip the cream to form soft peaks and set it aside.

Melt the chocolate over a bowl of simmering water, or in the microwave. If you're using the stovetop method, make sure the bottom of the bowl doesn't touch the hot water. Stir the chocolate until it's smooth and set it aside.

Place the egg, egg yolks and honey in a stainless steel bowl. Over a pan of simmering water, beat the mixture vigorously with a wire whisk until it thickens and turns light and pale. Gradually whisk this egg mixture into the melted chocolate. The chocolate will thicken at first, but as you keep adding and whisking, it will form a smooth, shiny mixture. Gently fold in the whipped cream until a light mixture forms. Add the rum and stir it in.

Pour this semifreddo into silicone moulds or six ½-cup ramekins. Alternatively, you can use a 3-cup loaf pan lined with plastic wrap.

Freeze overnight, covered.

To serve, place a small pile of chopped almonds on each plate.

Unmould the semifreddos and place 1 on each pile of almonds. If you're using ramekins, dip the bottom of each one in warm water, then run a paring knife around the edge of the ramekin to release the semifreddo. If you're using a loaf pan, turn it out onto a cutting board, remove the plastic wrap and cut a slice of semifreddo for each plate.

Decorate the semifreddo with the remaining almonds and serve.

To make life easier, you can unmould the semifreddos onto a parchment-lined baking sheet and put them back in the freezer a few hours before dinner.

CHOCOLATE ALMOND TORTE

Torta al Cioccolato

1½ cups almond meal (finely
   ground almonds)
¼ cup + 1 Tbsp all-purpose
   white flour
1 cup + 2 tsp granulated sugar
1 cup unsalted butter
15 oz good-quality dark
   chocolate, chopped (about
   2¾ cups)
6 eggs, separated
1 tsp salt
1 Tbsp Triple Sec or other
   orange-flavoured liqueur
Zest of 1 orange

This rich, chocolatey torte is heavenly served warm from the oven, and equally delicious at room temperature the next day. **Serves 6–8**

Preheat the oven to 350°F. Grease or spray a round 9- × 2½-inch cake or torte pan.

Measure the almond meal, flour and the 2 tsp of sugar into a bowl and whisk to combine. Set aside.

Cut the butter into several pieces. Melt the chocolate and butter in a large bowl set over a pan of simmering water or in the microwave. Stir until a smooth, shiny mixture forms. Set aside.

Beat the egg whites with ½ cup of the remaining sugar and the salt until medium peaks form. Set aside.

In a clean bowl, vigorously whisk the eggs yolks and the remaining ½ cup sugar over a pan of simmering water until they thicken and start to form a pale, light mixture—a sabayon.

Stir the flour and almond mixture into the melted chocolate. Whisk in the sabayon by hand, scraping the sides of the bowl to incorporate well. Stir in the orange liqueur and zest. Lastly, fold in the beaten egg whites, mixing gently until a smooth, light batter forms.

Scrape the batter into the prepared pan. Tap the pan on the counter a few times to eliminate any large air bubbles, then bake until the torte is puffed and its top is just starting to crack, 25 to 30 minutes.

Remove the torte from the oven, let it rest for 15 minutes, then gently unmould it while it's still slightly warm to let it cool evenly.

The torte can be served still warm from oven, or at room temperature. A dusting of icing sugar over the top and an espresso on the side is all you need to dress it up.

ALMOND LACE COOKIES

Biscotti alle Mandorle

½ cup granulated sugar
½ cup ground almonds
¼ cup unsalted butter
¼ cup light corn syrup
⅓ cup all-purpose white flour

These little cookies are the perfect accompaniment to Vin Santo dessert wine. Just dip the cookies into the sweet wine for a moment to soften them slightly then enjoy. It's just like dunking biscotti into coffee. **Makes 12 cookies**

Preheat the oven to 325°F, using the convection setting if possible. Line 2 baking trays with parchment paper.

Place the sugar, almonds, butter and corn syrup in a saucepan over medium heat just until the butter has melted. Stir in the flour.

Divide mixture in 12 equal spoonfuls over the prepared baking trays. Bake for 8 to 10 minutes, or until they're golden brown. Remove the cookies from the oven and let them sit for 1 to 2 minutes. Working quickly, shape each cookie around a wooden dowel into a cylinder, gently pressing the overlapped edge.

Store the cookies in an airtight container.

You can fill these with Chestnut Mousse (page 213) or serve as is.

CRUNCHY AMARETTI
Amaretti Croccanti

1 cup + 1 Tbsp marzipan,
  room temperature
¾ cup granulated sugar +
  1 cup for rolling cookies
2 Tbsp almond meal (also
  known as almond all-purpose
  white flour or almond meal)
2 egg whites
1 tsp amaretto

These delightful almond cookies are crunchy on the outside and chewy on the inside. Best served the day they're made, they're delicious with ice cream and perfect with a little amaretto. **Makes 24 bite-sized cookies**

In a stand mixer, or with handheld beaters, beat the marzipan, ¾ cup sugar and almond meal to combine them. The mixture will form small lumps. Add the egg whites and amaretto, and beat them for about 1 minute, scraping the sides of bowl, until the lumps disappear and a smooth paste forms.

Wrap this amaretti dough in plastic wrap and chill it for 3 hours or overnight. Preheat the oven to 350°F. Line 2 baking sheets with parchment paper.

When the dough has chilled and firmed up, roll it into balls the size of large walnuts. Drop the dough balls into a bowl filled with the remaining 1 cup sugar and roll them around to coat them thoroughly. Dip your fingers in cold water to keep the dough from sticking to your hands.

Place the balls on the prepared baking sheets 1 inch apart and bake, rotating the baking sheets 180 degrees halfway through the baking time, for about 15 minutes, or until the cookies are a light golden and cracking lightly on top.

Let the amaretti cool to room temperature before serving.

BISCOTTI | *Biscotti*

I love biscotti, and I really love crunchy, crunchy biscotti filled with nuts and chocolate. Here are two recipes—one for sophisticated, nutty pistachio biscotti, and one for a fun, chocolatey mocha version.

PISTACHIO BISCOTTI
Biscotti al Pistacchio

2 cups all-purpose white flour
1 cup granulated sugar
½ tsp baking powder
½ tsp baking soda
¼ tsp salt
3 eggs, beaten
1 tsp pure vanilla extract
½ tsp almond extract
    (optional)
1 cup coarsely chopped
    pistachios
Extra flour and sugar for rolling

Makes 40 small biscotti

Preheat the oven to 350°F. Line a baking tray with parchment paper or grease it thoroughly.

Place the flour, sugar, baking powder and soda and salt in a bowl or a mixer and stir to combine them.

Add the eggs all at once with the vanilla and almond extract, if using, and mix until the eggs just start to blend with the flour. Add the nuts and mix to form a smooth, slightly sticky dough.

Turn the dough out onto a clean, lightly floured surface and divide it in half. Roll each half into a narrow log, about 14 inches long, using as much flour as necessary to keep it from sticking. Roll the logs in sugar to coat them evenly then transfer them immediately to the prepared baking tray. Leave 3 inches between the logs.

Bake the logs until they're just firm and dry to the touch, about 25 minutes. Remove the tray from the oven and let cool for 5 minutes.

Gently transfer the logs to a cutting board 1 at a time, and slice them crosswise on a slight diagonal into about 20 even pieces.

Reduce the oven heat to 300°F.

Put the slices back on the tray, cut side down, and bake until all sides of the biscotti feel dry to the touch. To speed this process up, flip the biscotti over halfway through baking. This second baking stage can take 10 to 15 minutes for each side.

Serve biscotti with a big cup of coffee or a bowl of ice cream. They'll keep in an airtight container for up to 2 weeks.

MOCHA BISCOTTI

Biscotti Espressivi

2 cups all-purpose white flour
+ extra for rolling

1 cup granulated sugar + extra
for rolling

1 Tbsp + 1 tsp instant
espresso

1 tsp ground cinnamon

½ tsp baking powder

½ tsp baking soda

¼ tsp salt

3 eggs, beaten

1 tsp pure vanilla extract

½ cup chopped (around the
size of chocolate chips)
dark chocolate

½ cup chopped (around the
size of chocolate chips)
milk chocolate

Makes 40 small biscotti

Preheat the oven to 350°F. Line a baking tray with parchment paper or grease it thoroughly.

Place the flour, sugar, espresso powder, cinnamon, baking powder and soda and salt in a bowl or a mixer and stir to combine them.

Add the eggs all at once with the vanilla, and mix until the eggs just start to blend with the flour. Add the dark and milk chocolate and mix to form a smooth, slightly sticky dough.

Turn the dough out onto a clean, lightly floured surface and divide it in half. Roll each half into a narrow log, about 14 inches long, using as much flour as necessary to keep it from sticking. Roll the logs in sugar to coat them evenly then transfer them immediately to the prepared baking sheet. Leave 3 inches between the logs.

Bake the logs until they're just firm and dry to the touch, about 25 minutes. Remove the trays from the oven and let cool for 5 minutes.

Gently transfer the logs to a cutting board 1 at a time, and slice them crosswise on a slight diagonal into about 20 even pieces.

Reduce the oven heat to 300°F.

Put the slices back on the tray, cut side down, and bake until all sides of the biscotti feel dry to the touch. To speed this process up, flip the biscotti over halfway through baking. This second baking stage can take 10 to 15 minutes for each side.

Serve biscotti with a big cup of coffee or a bowl of ice cream. They'll keep in an airtight container for up to 2 weeks.

SWEET ALMOND AND PINE NUT BREAD
Pan Dolce

3¼ tsp active dry (not instant)
    yeast (or 1½ packets)

3 Tbsp lukewarm water

1 cup + 1 tsp granulated
    sugar, divided

2⅔ cups all-purpose white
    flour

½ tsp salt

4 eggs

⅔ cup melted butter

Zest of 1 orange

Zest of 1 lemon

2 Tbsp orange flower water
    (optional)

1 cup whole, blanched
    almonds

1 cup pine nuts

1 egg yolk, beaten, for glazing

2 Tbsp coarse sugar (turbinado
    or "sugar in the raw") for
    sprinkling (optional)

This rich, golden bread is chock full of toasty almonds and pine nuts, with a lovely orange scent. It's equally delicious sliced warm from the oven with creamy cheeses and fruit, or toasted the next day with apricot jam. **Serves 6–8**

Dissolve the yeast in the lukewarm water, sprinkle it with the 1 tsp of sugar and let it proof in a warm place until the mixture foams and the yeast rises to the top, about 10 minutes.

Using a stand mixer, or handheld beaters, stir the flour, salt and 1 cup sugar together. Add the eggs 1 at a time, mixing thoroughly between additions, the melted butter and the yeast mixture to form a soft dough. Add the orange and lemon zests, and orange flower water, if using.

Scrape the dough into an oiled bowl, cover it with a damp cloth or plastic wrap and let it rise in a warm place until it's doubled in volume, about 2 hours.

Preheat the oven to 350°F.

On a rimmed baking sheet, toast the almonds lightly until they're a pale, golden colour, about 10 to 12 minutes. Remove them from the oven and cool.

Line a baking sheet with parchment paper or oil it thoroughly.

Once the dough has risen, knead it (oil your hands if the dough is still sticky), with just enough flour to keep it from sticking, a few times until it's smooth and soft. Knead in the toasted almonds and pine nuts.

Roll the dough on a clean, lightly floured surface to form a long, thin rope. Transfer it to the prepared baking sheet and form it into a circle, 10 to 12 inches in diameter, pinching the ends of the rope together. Brush the dough with the egg yolk and sprinkle it all over with the coarse sugar, if using.

Let it rise for 1 hour, or until the dough springs back after being gently pushed with a finger.

Preheat the oven to 375°F.

Bake the loaf until it's a deep golden colour and it sounds hollow when tapped, about 30 minutes. Remove the loaf from the oven and let it cool on a rack.

Serve this bread warm or cool. It will keep for 3 to 4 days, wrapped, at room temperature, and toasting does wonders to bring it back to life!

OLIVE OIL AND GRAPE CAKE
WITH HONEYED MASCARPONE AND PINE NUTS

Torta Mariella

OLIVE OIL AND GRAPE CAKE

¾ cup + 1 Tbsp all-purpose
  white flour
½ tsp baking powder
Pinch salt
2 whole large eggs
¾ cup granulated sugar
½ cup extra virgin olive oil
⅓ cup sherry (such as Tio
  Pepe)
1 tsp pure vanilla extract
2 cups coronation grapes
3 Tbsp toasted pine nuts

HONEYED MASCARPONE

1 cup mascarpone cheese
½ cup whipping cream
3 Tbsp liquid honey

This cake is light and moist, with great olive oil flavour. It's a wonderful way to take advantage of the coronation grape season, and the sherry baked into the batter really brings out the winey flavour of the grapes. **Serves 6**

Preheat the oven to 350°F. Spray or grease 6 individual cake rings, or 1 shallow 9-inch straight-sided round cake or torte pan. A springform pan is not suitable for this recipe. If you're using a 9-inch pan, line the bottom of it with parchment paper if you prefer. If you're using rings, set them on a parchment-paper-lined baking sheet.

Sift the flour and baking powder with the pinch of salt. Set aside.

Using a stand mixer, or handheld beaters, beat the eggs, sugar and olive oil until light. The oil and eggs will emulsify quickly to make a beautiful light, fluffy, yellow batter. Add half the sherry and the vanilla, and beat to combine. Add half the reserved flour mixture all at once, and beat until just incorporated. Add the remaining sherry and beat well. Add the remaining flour mixture and beat on low speed to lighten the batter, about 45 seconds.

Divide the batter between the 6 cake rings, or scrape it into the single cake pan. Generously sprinkle the grapes over the surface of the batter.

Bake the cake until it's golden all over, 50 to 55 minutes. The grapes will sink to the bottom, so you may want to move the tray down to the bottom rack halfway through baking to ensure the cake cooks through. Insert a cake tester or toothpick to test if the cake is cooked through.

Remove the cake from the oven, rest it for 10 minutes then gently unmould it onto a cooling rack while it's still warm. Let it cool on the rack.

For the honeyed mascarpone, simply whip together all the ingredients until they're thick and holding soft peaks.

Serve the olive oil cake warm (you can warm it through again in a 350°F oven if necessary), topped with a dollop of honeyed mascarpone and sprinkled with the toasted pine nuts.

MENUS
Il Menú

FAMILY TRADITIONS
Tradizione della Famiglia

58   **FIGS WITH GOAT CHEESE AND PROSCIUTTO**
Try a light white wine with no oak. Goat cheese has a strong capric acid that is best matched with Sauvignon Blanc.

17   **MEAT SAUCE**
This classic Italian pasta needs an Italian wine. In Tuscany you can find a wine called Vino Nobile di Montepulciano. It's made with a grape called *prugnolo pentille*, which is a hybrid of Sangiovese and tends to have a little more body than its cousin that you find in Chianti. It offers a great match for the meat sauce.

175, 190   **NONNO'S MEATBALLS WITH EDITH'S BROCCOLI**
Nonno's Meatballs and Edith's Broccoli are also great with Vino Nobile di Montepulciano. One of my favourite, more consistent Vino Nobiles is the Avignonesi 2003, one of the best vintages they've had in recent years.

214   **CRÈME CARAMEL**
A sweet dessert wine could work fine with this but a coffee drink is even better. Try Bailey's and "butter ripple snaps" mixed in hot coffee and topped with whipped cream.

MAMMA-NONNA EDITH'S DINNER
La Cena di Mamma-Nonna Edith

34   **CAPRESE SALAD**
25   **MINESTRONE**
180   **EDITH'S STUFFED RED BELL PEPPERS**
212   **VANILLA BEAN PANNACOTTA WITH FRESH BERRIES**

Well, if I were to serve dinner to Nonna Edith I can assure you that all she would want to drink is sparkling wine. Starting with Prosecco for the caprese, moving on to Champagne for the main course and finishing with Moscato d'Asti for dessert.

ANTONIO'S FAVOURITES
Favoriti di Antonio

140 **SPOT PRAWNS IN VERMOUTH SAUCE**
Start this meal with a sparkling wine to complement the spot prawns. Italy makes many different styles of sparkling but our favourite is Franciacorta. Bellavista is a great producer of this varietal. Otherwise an aromatic white like Viognier is a nice choice.

137 **MUSSELS IN RED SAUCE**
Red or white — it's really up to you. White wine is probably what most sommeliers would suggest, but if you prefer red, it can work too. The tomatoes introduce a lot of acidity and a light Sangiovese will cut through that acidity, making both the wine and tomatoes taste sweeter.

71 **SPAGHETTI QUATTRO**
An all-time favourite at the restaurants, Spaghetti Quattro is hot and spicy. If you want to mellow out the heat, Vernaccia di San Gimignano from Tuscany has the perfect minerality to hold up to the garlic and beans. But if you like it hot, choose a bold Tuscan red from the region of Bolgheri.

183 **TRIPE WITH PANCETTA**
An earthy Tuscan red wine like Brunello di Montalcino enhances the flavor of the *trippa*.

222 **PISTACHIO BISCOTTI**
Dip your biscotti in Vin Santo dessert wine made from dried, late-harvest grapes.

ROMAN FEAST
La Festa Romana

54	**BEEF CARPACCIO**
34	**CAPRESE SALAD**
104	**CHICKEN ROTOLO**

For the first two courses, white is a must. Sparkling wine could work, but I prefer a dry acidic white like Sauvignon Blanc or Sémillon. Be sure to pick one from the old world like France or Italy as other wines may be too fruity. For the Chicken Rotolo you'll want to start with a lighter red like Pinot Noir but Barbaresco is also perfect.

178, 201 BEEF TENDERLOIN WITH AGED BALSAMIC SERVED WITH WILD MUSHROOM RAGOUT

With the beef tenderloin you want a wine with more body and structure. Try Farnito Cabernet Sauvignon from Tuscany. It's a good choice thanks to its earthy flavour, which pairs well with the mushroom sauce. It would be more difficult to pair this dish with a new world Cabernet Sauvignon, which often has fruit like cherry and cassis.

212 VANILLA BEAN PANNACOTTA WITH FRESH BERRIES

If you're up for it a light dessert wine like Moscato d'Asti would finish the feast nicely.

LUNCH IN ROME
Il Pranzo a Roma

Colli Albani, an Italian Sauvignon Blanc, or any other light white wine is a good match for the Swordfish Carpaccio and the clams.

For the pasta, you should move on to red wine. Try a light Sangiovese like Rosso di Montalcino.

Amarone from Valpolicella offers the perfect pairing for the figs in the sauce.

Tiramisu means "pick me up." Try a cocktail with the same name. Mix equal parts of Baileys, Kahlúa and espresso over ice. *Perfetto*!

PICNIC PARTY
Scampagnata

62	**OLIVE TAPENADE CROSTINI**
37	**CUCUMBER SALAD**
141	**POACHED OCTOPUS WITH CANNELLINI BEANS**
170	**VEAL MEDALLIONS IN A TUNA AND CAPER SAUCE**
221	**CRUNCHY AMARETTI**

Your favourite Pinot Grigio will go very well with everything on this menu.
Nice and simple: exactly right for a picnic.

SPORTS MATCH
Serata Sportiva

62	**ASSORTED CROSTINI**
55	**STEAK TARTARE**

Let's be honest here—if you call the boys over to watch the big game, beer has to
be on the menu. A big bucket filled with ice and Peroni beer is a very civilized way
to start the afternoon.

90   BAKED RIGATONI

By the time the Baked Rigatoni comes out, your friends, especially the Italian
ones, are going to be looking for a glass of red wine. A simple Chianti is the best
way to keep everybody interested in the game.

150   DRUNKEN CHICKEN

Step it up a little here: Chianti Classico Riserva.

65   SEMOLINA CRACKERS WITH ASSORTED CHEESES

You can stay with wine for the cheese. But not all cheese matches with red wine.
Here's a simple rule to follow: the harder the cheese the better it tastes with red
wine. If you like strong blue cheese, try vintage port for a classic pairing.

BIG BOYS' FEAST
La Grande Abbuffata

47 **GRILLED CALAMARI STEAK**
195 **EGGPLANT WITH FONTINA CHEESE**
55 **STEAK TARTARE**

These three dishes call for a white wine. Yes, even the Steak Tartare. A good unoaked white like Arneis from Piedmont is perfect.

102 **BRAISED RABBIT CANNELLONI**
You'll want to visit Tuscany for this dish. Choose Brunello to go with the earthy flavour of the beans and elegant flavour of the rabbit. It's a match made in heaven.

172 **CORSI OSSO BUCO**
Stick with the Brunello, or if you want a little more body, Guado al Tasso from Bolgheri, Tuscany, is even better.

225 **SWEET ALMOND AND PINE NUT BREAD**
A little digestive like amaretto on the rocks works well here, but if you want to stay in the wine world try Reciotto. It's a red dessert wine from the Veneto region that is nuttier than white dessert wine.

LADIES' LUNCH
Il Pranzo delle Signore

200 **BAKED MUSHROOMS**
38 **CHICKEN SALAD WITH ARUGULA**
204 **PHYLLO, SOUR CHERRY AND MASCARPONE TOWERS**

With this menu you want to treat yourself with a bright and lively white wine. British Columbia offers great fruit-forward, aromatic whites like Pinot Blanc, which works perfectly with the arugula. Otherwise, an international Viognier is also a great match for this menu.

LATE-NIGHT SUPPER
Alle Ore Piccole

28   **SMOKED CHICKEN, CORN AND POTATO CHOWDER**
78   **SPAGHETTI WITH OLIVE OIL AND GARLIC**
200   **BAKED MUSHROOMS**

Let's face it — it's late. A simple glass or two of Barbera d'Alba, Sovrana from Batasiolo, is just what you need. It'll pair perfectly with the Baked Mushrooms and won't overpower the chowder or the pasta.

FROM THE SEA
Tutto Mare

43   **DUNGENESS CRAB AND SEA SCALLOP CAKES**
Start with sparkling. A yeasty Champagne is nice, and goes well with the bread-crumbs on the crab and scallop cakes.

118   **SALMON FILLET WITH HONEY**
An unoaked white is ideal with the salmon because oak tends to make salmon taste very fishy. Or try Gavi di Gavi from Piedmont. Chablis, a lesser-oaked Chardonnay, is also nice.

124   **PISTACHIO-CRUSTED ORANGE ROUGHY WITH FIRE-ROASTED PEPPER SAUCE**
On the other hand, this dish calls for an oaky Chardonnay. Planeta Chardonnay from Sicily is a good as it gets.

222   **PISTACHIO BISCOTTI**
Finish the meal with a Vin Santo for dipping.

COLD WINTER NIGHT

Una Sera d' Inverno

24   **BREAD SOUP**

115   **SEARED POLENTA**

77   **SPAGHETTI CARBONARA**

A full-body white like Chardonnay is a safe choice for this menu. If you want to be a little more adventurous, Gavi di Gavi from Piedmont is a fantastic white, especially with the carbonara sauce.

182   **SAUSAGE AND BEANS**

Beans always call for a Sangiovese from Tuscany. And the spicier the sausages, the lighter the wine should be — Chianti Classico is great.

213   **CHESTNUT MOUSSE**

Barolo Chinato is a spicy and nutty dessert wine from the northwest of Italy and would be great with this dessert.

HOT SUMMER NIGHT

Una Sera d' Estate

30   **GREEN SALAD WITH GOAT CHEESE AND APPLES**

You must start with Sauvignon Blanc for the goat cheese, and the fruitier the better here. Something from New Zealand with bright acidity and gooseberry flavours is perfect for the apples.

127   **AHI TUNA WITH ANGEL HAIR PASTA**

196   **EGGPLANT BOATS**

You can stay with the same wine for this and the next course, but a wine with less fruit like Pinot Gris or Chardonnay will give a little more body for the seafood.

207   **BANANA RASPBERRY SUNDAE**

Fruit wines are rapidly gaining in popularity, and a raspberry wine would be perfect here. Alternatively, Bonny Doon in California makes a digestif called Framboise that's just delicious.

ITALIANS INVADE VANCOUVER

L'Italia invade Vancouver

50 **MUSHROOM CARPACCIO**
Mushroom Carpaccio is very delicately flavoured and a light white like Soave from the Northeast of Italy would be perfect.

58 **FIGS WITH GOAT CHEESE AND PROSCIUTTO**
Try Moscato d'Asti and score extra points from your friends for stepping away from conventional wines. This is guaranteed to be a successful pairing.

73 **PINE MUSHROOM SPAGHETTI**
This earthy pasta needs an earthy wine from Piedmont. Barbera is still light enough to keep the focus on the mushrooms and is the best way to prepare you for the next course. Try La Spinetta "Pin," a Nebbiolo and Barbera blend.

176, 192 **BAROLO-MARINATED BEEF TENDERLOIN SERVED WITH GREEN BEANS WITH TOMATO**
You guessed it! Use the same wine in the sauce as you're planning to serve your guests at dinner. It's a taste experience you have to try at least once in your life.

210 **RED WINE SORBET WITH HONEY TUILES**
Try Lambrusco—it's a slightly sparkling semi-sweet red wine from the Lombardy region.

BAPTISM OF THE TWO STARS

Battesimo delle due Stelle

52 RADICCHIO WITH FRESH MOZZARELLA
Brachetto d'Acqui from Piedmont, a light, almost sweet, usually *frizzante* red wine, is the perfect pairing for this dish. A sweet white such as Riesling works well too.

85 FETTUCCINE WITH MUSHROOMS
Stay in the region of Piedmont with a full-bodied Chardonnay for this dish. Our favourite is Rossj-Bass by Angelo Gaja.

174 GRILLED VEAL T-BONE WITH GRANNY SMITH APPLES
Piedmont is emerging as a theme for this menu and the big, high-acidity and high-tannin Nebbiolo from Barolo works great for red meat while the apple sauce is the perfect pairing for Barolo.

219 CHOCOLATE ALMOND TORTE
A sweet Moscadello for this one, the older the better to pair with the almonds.

METRIC CONVERSIONS

VOLUME

⅛ tsp	0.5 mL
¼ tsp	1 mL
½ tsp	2 mL
¾ tsp	4 mL
1 tsp	5 mL
1½ tsp	7.5 mL
2 tsp	10 mL
1 Tbsp	15 mL
2 Tbsp	30 mL
3 Tbsp	45 mL
¼ cup	60 mL
⅓ cup	80 mL
½ cup	125 mL
⅔ cup	160 mL
¾ cup	185 mL
1 cup	250 mL
1¼ cups	310 mL
1½ cups	375 mL
1¾ cups	435 mL
2 cups	500 mL
3 cups	750 mL
4 cups	1 L
6 cups	1.5 L
7 cups	1.75 L
8 cups	2 L
10 cups	2.5 L
12 cups	3 L
16 cups	4 L
20 cups	5 L
24 cups	6 L

WEIGHT

¼ oz	7 g
1 oz	30 g
2 oz	60 g
3 oz	90 g
3½ oz	100 g
4 oz	125 g
¼ lb	125 g
5 oz	150 g
6 oz	175 g
7 oz	200 g
8 oz	250 g
½ lb	250 g
10 oz	300 g
¾ lb	375 g
12 oz	375 g
14 oz	400 g
1 lb	460 g
18 oz	510 g
1½ lb	750 g
2 lb	1 kg
3 lb	1.5 kg
4 lb	1.8 kg
5 lb	2.2 kg
6 lb	2.7 kg

PAN, LOAF AND DISH SIZES

8-inch square	20 cm square (2 L)
9-inch round	23 cm round (1.5 L)
9- × 5-inch	23 × 12 cm (2 L)
9- × 13-inch	23 × 33 cm (3.5 L)

LENGTH

⅛ inch	3 mm
¼ inch	6 mm
½ inch	1 cm
¾ inch	2 cm
1 inch	2.5 cm
1½ inches	4 cm
2 inches	5 cm
2½ inches	6 cm
3 inches	8 cm
4 inches	10 cm
4½ inches	11 cm
5 inches	12 cm
6 inches	15 cm
7 inches	18 cm
8 inches	20 cm
8½ inches	22 cm
9 inches	23 cm
10 inches	25 cm
11 inches	28 cm
12 inches	30 cm
13 inches	33 cm
17 inches	43 cm
20 inches	50 cm

TEMPERATURE

130°F	54°C
135°F	57°C
145°F	63°C
150°F	66°C
160°F	71°C
165°F	74°C
170°F	77°C
300°F	150°C
325°F	160°C
350°F	180°C
375°F	190°C
400°F	200°C
425°F	220°C
450°F	230°C
500°F	260°C

CAN SIZES

6 oz	170 g
12 oz	355 mL
14 oz	398 mL
28 oz	796 mL
100 oz	2.84 L

INDEX

ACKNOWLEDGEMENTS
Ringraziamenti

Writing this cookbook was a collaborative effort and a major undertaking. If only we'd known! We couldn't have done it without the support of our families especially Edith and Ida, Tanis's beloved Alex, Leo and Evan Tsisserev, as well as her own Italian mother, Erin, and a few other special people in particular.

Jeremie Trottier from Quattro at Whistler is an incredible chef and an even more incredible friend. Jeremie, thank you for all your support with this project and more importantly your friendship over the years.

Many of the desserts in this book come courtesy of a terrific pastry chef, Merri Schwartz (see pages 208, 210, 212, 216, 219, 221, 222, 224 and 225). Not only is Merri a talented pastry chef, she is also founder and director of *Growing Chefs! Chefs for Children's Urban Agriculture.*

We owe a heartfelt thank you to Joan Cross who meticulously tested every recipe in this book to ensure it translated well from my mind, to the page, to your belly. Joan is an extremely talented cook and a pleasure to know.

To Luc Trottier of Quattro at Whistler for his input on the wines.

Some of the recipes in this book have been around for generations on scraps of worn paper, or floating around in my mind, and never written down. Sheila MacLean, from Quattro at Whistler, typed them up for me. *Grazie*, Sheila!

Quattro has worked with photographer Hamid Attie for years and when it came time to select a photographer for this book, we didn't consider anyone else.

To my nephew, Gio Corsi, for sharing a favourite family memory in this book.

To my beautiful family: Mario, Gina, Gio and Michelle Corsi; Ida Corsi; Stefano, Ginevra, Chiara and Ludovica Giardini; Sara Serafini; Paolo, Filippo, Iacopo and Beatrice Bedeschi; Giulia Giardini; Pietro, Janis and Isabella Giardini; Maurizio, Maru and Sabrina Corsi; Massimo Corsi; Antonella Grassi; Claudio and Andrea Corsi; Antonella Tiberi; and of course Ida, Albert, Sofia and Amaya Aiello; and Patrick and Edith Corsi.

I hope you create as many wonderful memories while enjoying the recipes in this book as my family has.

— ANTONIO CORSI